Henry Stanley

and the Quest for the Source of the Nile

Henry Stanley

and the Quest for the Source of the Nile

by Daniel Cohen

M Evans

Lanham • New York • Boulder • Toronto • Plymouth, UK

To Jim and Candy Hinckley

M. Evans
An imprint of The Rowman & Littlefield Publishing Group, Inc.
4501 Forbes Boulevard, Suite 200, Lanham, Maryland 20706
http://www.rlpgtrade.com

10 Thornbury Road, Plymouth PL6 7PP, United Kingdom

Distributed by National Book Network

British Library Cataloguing in Publication Information Available

Library of Congress Cataloging-in-Publication Data Available

ISBN 13: 978-1-59077-348-2(pbk: alk. paper)

☉™ The paper used in this publication meets the minimum requirements of American National Standard for Information Sciences—Permanence of Paper for Printed Library Materials, ANSI/NISO Z39.48-1992.

Printed in the United States of America

Design by Lauren Dong

Contents

The African Expeditions of Henry Stanley

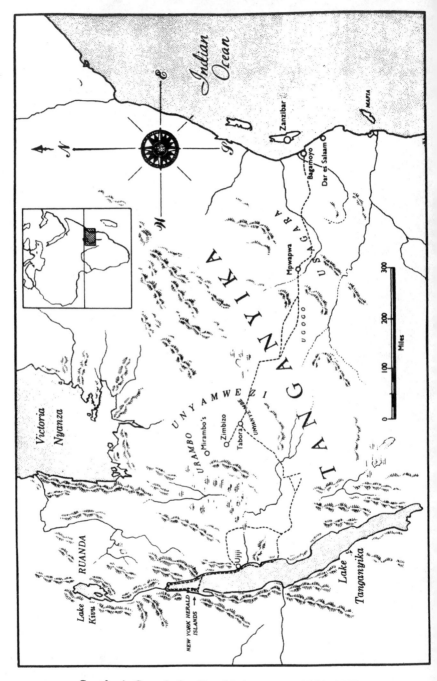

Stanley's Search for Dr. Livingstone, 1871–1872

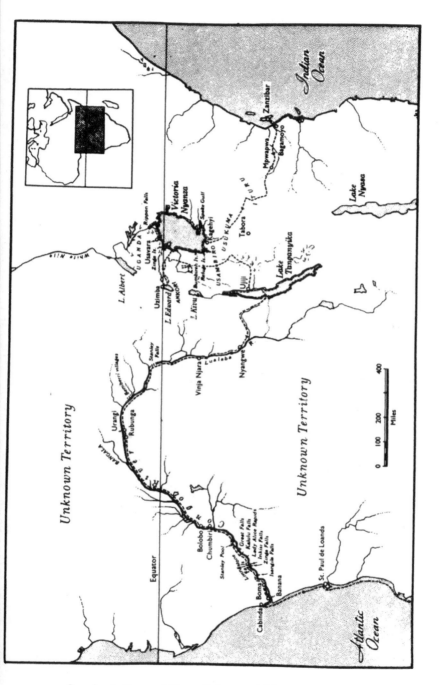

Stanley's Second Expedition to Africa, 1874–1877

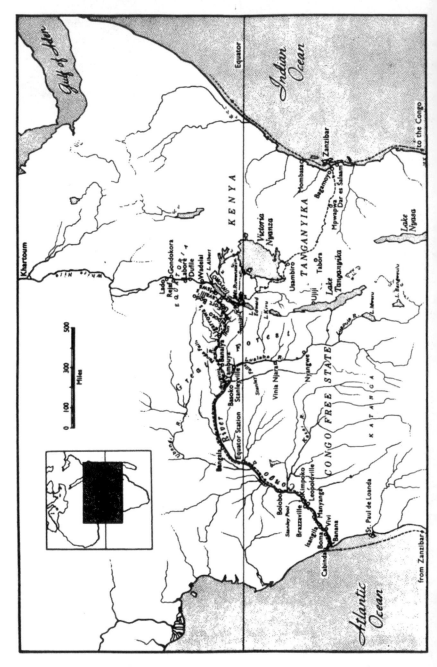

The Route of the Emin Pasha Relief Expedition Across Central
Africa, 1887–1889

Author's Note

Unless otherwise attributed, all quotations and dialogue in this book have been taken directly from the writings of Henry Stanley. A list of his works is given in the bibliography.

CHAPTER 1

The Mountains of the Moon

"No unexplored region in our times, neither the heights of the Himalayas, the Antarctic wastes, nor even the hidden side of the moon, has excited quite the same fascination as the mystery of the sources of the Nile. For two thousand years at least the problem was debated and remained unsolved. . . . By the middle of the nineteenth century . . . this matter had become . . . 'the greatest geographical secret after the discovery of America.'" So begins Alan Moorehead's classic *The White Nile*.

It is not hard to understand why the unknown source of the Nile fascinated people. The Nile is the basis of life in Egypt, home of one of the oldest, most powerful, and most exotic of all ancient civilizations. Without the Nile there could have been no Pyramids, no Sphinx, no civilization at all in Egypt, for it almost never rains there, and agriculture depends entirely on water drawn from the river and particularly on the annual flood that renews both the moisture and the soil of the Nile Delta. If the flood failed for a single year, Egypt would perish. But it has never failed, not once in thousands of years of recorded history. And the flood rises during the driest and hottest time of the year.

Where does all that water come from?

The Nile flows north from the center of Africa through more than a thousand miles of hot, rainless desert. The source of the Nile clearly lay somewhere in the middle of the African continent, but all attempts to find the place where the great river began proved to be incredibly difficult. Going upriver, against the current, was hard enough, particularly in the days before steam power. There was the heat of the desert and the great rapids, or cataracts, of the Nile to be passed. And if these difficulties could be overcome, there was the impassable barrier of the Sudd.

In the southern part of the Sudan the air grows more humid, and the banks of the Nile are green year round. Soon the traveler finds that the river has merged with a huge swamp that is the Sudd. There is no clear channel through this vast region of weed-choked muddy water. The swamp is the home for the hippopotamus, the crocodile, and clouds of disease-bearing mosquitoes. Many travelers had tried to trace the course of the river through the Sudd—none had succeeded. The great swamp was impenetrable.

Another approach to finding the source of the Nile was to march inland from either the east or west coast of Africa right to the heart of the continent. But this required a march of hundreds of miles through hostile and completely unknown territory, for up until the middle of the last century the center of Africa was just a big blank marked "unexplored" on the world's maps. How could any explorer be sure that he had really found the source of the Nile? Aside from the enormous difficulties of African exploration, there were endless bitter disputes over the significance of different discoveries.

Yet the source of the Nile was not truly unknown; someone had once known the source, but that knowledge had been lost. There was a widely repeated story that in the first century A.D. a Greek merchant named Diogenes landed on the coast of Africa and, according to his own account, "travelled inland for a 25-days journey and arrived in the vicinity of two great lakes and the snowy range of mountains whence the Nile draws its twin sources." In the second century A.D., the great Egyptian geographer Ptolemy drew a famous map of Africa that showed the Nile originating in two lakes that were in turn watered from a high range of mountains, the *Lunae Montes*, the Mountains of the Moon.

Vague reports of snow-capped mountains in Central Africa had filtered out of the unknown interior for a long time. But most nineteenth-century geographers refused to believe such reports, because the existence of unmelted snow so close to the equator seemed ridiculous. Yet the snow-capped Mountains of the Moon that are the ultimate source of the Nile do exist. The man who first brought credible reports of the mountains to the outside world was the greatest of all African explorers, Henry Morton Stanley.

Like other African explorers of the nineteenth century, Stanley too had taken part in the great quest for the source of the Nile. Yet when he found the Mountains of the Moon he was not really looking for them. It was 1889, and Stanley was on his last, strangest, and most terrifying African journey. He had faced extreme hardships before, but nothing matched the horrors of the

Ituri Forest. There were starvation, disease, ghastly accidents, and almost constant attack from hidden Pygmy
enemies. His men were dropping around Stanley at a
frightful rate. Those who didn't actually die were usually
too starved and sick to move. Stanley himself was often
driven half mad with pain or was delirious with fever.
Yet somehow he persevered and broke out of the forest.
On April 20, 1889, the advance party of Stanley's expedition reported seeing a white mountain. A month later
Stanley himelf saw the mountain, or more accurately a
whole range of snow-capped mountains, on the equator
in the heart of tropical Africa! It was then that Stanley
realized that he had found the fabled Mountains of the
Moon, the ultimate source of the Nile.

Other travelers had passed close enough to the Mountains of the Moon, or Ruwenzori, as they were called, to
see them. But somehow mists or clouds had always ob-
scured the mountains. The mists cleared for Stanley. He
had always felt that his life had been guided by some sort
of special Providence—this was just another example of
it.

Stanley can be excused for believing in special Providence. His own life was so improbable that it is hard to
believe. It could have been dreamed up by a collabora-
tion of Charles Dickens and Edgar Rice Burroughs.

Stanley became one of the most famous men of his
day. Everyone in Europe and America knew of his ex-
ploits. His African nickname Bula Matari—"breaker of
rocks"—was known from one end of Africa to the other.
There was a mountain, a lake, even a city named after
him.

But as time passes, conditions and attitudes change.
The Africa that Stanley explored is now made up of
independent nations that have a different perspective on

history and their own set of heroes. Much of what Stanley believed he accomplished has crumbled, and many of the values that he held have proved false. As a result a name that was once instantly recognizable in Chicago, London, or the Congo, is now little remembered. But no change in attitude, historical perspective, or values can erase the wild adventure, heroic courage, and sheer improbability of the life of Henry Morton Stanley.

CHAPTER 2

John Rowlands

It has been said that no other famous public man of his time started so low in life and rose so high as Stanley. Certainly no one started so low.

In the beginning there was no Henry Morton Stanley. On January 28, 1841, Miss Elizabeth Parry of the town of Denbigh in northern Wales gave birth to a son. He was baptized John Rowlands—presumably the name of his father, who may have died shortly after the boy's birth, though no one knows for sure. Elizabeth then ran off to London, leaving the infant in the care of her father, Moses Parry. He had once been reasonably prosperous but had fallen on hard times and was reduced to working in the local slaughterhouse. Old Moses died when the boy was about four, and his care was passed on to a couple of uncles who boarded him out with an old couple named Price. That arrangement lasted for about two years until the uncles stopped paying the boy's modest boarding expenses. It was then that Dick Price, son of the couple who had been boarding the boy, took him for a long walk.

John was told that he was being taken to see his Aunt Mary. He was taken instead to a large stone building surrounded by an iron fence. Dick rang the bell, and as an adult Stanley recalled:

"A somber-faced stranger appeared at the door, who despite my remonstrances seized me by the hand, and drew me within, while Dick tried to soothe my fears with glib promises that he was only going to bring my Aunt Mary to me. The door closed on him, and, with the echoing sound, I experienced for the first time the awful feeling of utter desolateness."

The boy had been taken to the St. Asaph Union Workhouse. The workhouse was an institution in Victorian England where those too poor, too young, too old, or too ill to care for themselves were kept in prisonlike conditions. The purpose of such institutions was to get the poor out of sight and to keep them from starving and begging along the roadside.

"At six in the morning they are all roused from sleep; and at 8 o'clock at night they are penned up in their dormitories. Bread, gruel, rice, and potatoes compose principally their fare, after being nicely weighed and measured. On Saturdays each person must undergo a thorough scrubbing, and on Sundays they must submit to two sermons, which treat of things never practiced, and patiently kneel during a prayer as long as a sermon, in the evening.

"It is a fearful fate, that of a British outcast, because the punishment afflicts the mind and breaks the heart. . . ."

It was doubly fearful for young Rowlands because he

was put in the charge of the schoolmaster James Francis, an embittered one-handed ex-miner given to savage, even insane, rages. Indeed, Francis was finally carted off to the madhouse where he died—but that came too late to do young Rowlands any good. Francis beat his charges with his cane or a birch rod, kicked and punched them, and threw them down on the stone floor, for the most trivial of offenses. Rowlands received his first severe beating from Francis for being unable to pronounce the name "Joseph" properly in Bible class.

The most popular boy in the workhouse was an amiable dark-haired lad named Willie Roberts. He was Rowlands's friend and idol. Then one day Willie was gone, and there was a rumor that he had died suddenly. Rowlands and some of the other boys sneaked into the "deadhouse" and found Willie's body laid out on a black bier and covered by a sheet. When the sheet was drawn aside they found the body was a mass of sores, cuts, and bruises. The boys were convinced that Willie had been beaten to death by the sadistic Francis.

The children of the workhouse were supposed to be trained in useful trades—in practice they were put to work doing simple tasks like cleaning the grounds and washing the floors. Education consisted primarily of memorizing long passages from the Bible or other religious texts. The sexes in the workhouse were strictly segregated; Rowlands had no notion of sex and only the foggiest conception of family life, since none of his family ever visited him.

"I must have been twelve ere I knew that a mother was indispensable to every child."

One day Francis came to him during dinner, the one time of day when all the inmates were gathered together, and pointed out a tall woman with an oval face and a coil of dark hair, and asked if he recognized her.

"No, sir," the boy replied.

"What, do you not know your own mother?"

John glanced at the woman and she regarded him "with a look of cool, critical scrutiny. I had expected to feel a gush of tenderness towards her, but her expression was so chilling that the valves of my heart closed as with a snap."

Elizabeth Parry had married a man named Jones and had brought with her to the workhouse a young boy and girl. She left after a few weeks, taking the boy with her but leaving the girl, Emma. Emma was listed in the records as a "deserted bastard." Owing to the strict segregation of sexes John never was able to speak to his half sister. When she was fourteen, Emma left the workhouse to become a servant.

There was not much room for individuality in a workhouse, but John Rowlands did manage to stand out a bit. He was good at drawing and singing, and he had an exceptional memory. When the government inspector visited St. Asaph, he declared John to be "the most advanced pupil." The local bishop gave him an autographed Bible—a prized possession that he carried with him for years. The religious principles that were literally beaten into his head in the workhouse stayed with him for life.

The years spent in the workhouse gave a permanent shape and texture to the future explorer's personality. He was immune to hardship and loneliness—nothing he faced in Africa as an adult was harder or more frightening than his life as a child in St. Asaph. The workhouse also left him isolated from and suspicious of all other human beings. Physically and mentally he was extremely tough, yet he was also abnormally touchy and sensitive to every slight—real and imagined. One of the things John was sensitive about was his appearance. He was short, with a dark complexion, and despite the meager workhouse food, he was quite fat as a boy. He could never forget someone telling him he looked "prime for eating."

Rowlands was not a particularly rebellious child, until one day, when he was fifteen, the sadistic Francis went too far and drove him to strike back. "But for the stupid and brutal scene which brought it about I might eventually have been apprenticed to some trade or another, and would have mildewed in Wales. . . ."

A new table had been ordered for the school and someone had scratched it. This drove Francis into one of his insane rages. He demanded to know the culprit, and when no one stepped forward, he threatened to flog the entire class and proceeded to do just that. But when he reached John, the boy suddenly and quite unexpectedly refused to submit.

Francis grabbed him by the collar, threw him on the bench, and began punching him. John kicked back at his tormentor and, "by chance, the booted foot smashed his glasses, and almost blinded him with their splinters. Starting backward with the excruciating pain, he contrived to stumble over a bench, and the back of his head struck the stone floor. . . ." John grabbed Francis's stick and began to beat him as he lay on the floor.

When his fury subsided John felt more puzzled than anything else. What was he to do now? Had he killed Francis? If not, could he possibly submit to the beating that would surely follow once the master recovered? The boys dragged the limp form of Francis back to his study. One of John's friends, a lad named Mose, suggested that the both of them should run away. "I was in a mood to listen to the promptings." But before he left, he sent a boy to check on Francis's condition—the master had regained consciousness and was washing the blood from his face.

John and Mose left the workhouse immediately. "We climbed over the garden-wall and dropped into Conway's field, and thence hastened through the high corn . . . as though pursued by bloodhounds." The first few hours of freedom were filled with joy and anticipation, but reality soon asserted itself. The boys had no money and no food. With their close-cropped hair and workhouse uniforms they were clearly outcasts and were treated as such by practically everyone they met. They finally decided it would be best to go to Denbigh, where Mose's family lived. There they were greeted warmly. Mose's mother knew something of Rowlands's family— she had been a servant in the house of old Moses Parry in the days when he had money. John was told that his father had died years earlier, but that his paternal grandfather, also named John Rowlands, was prosperous and lived nearby. But she warned there was "little hope of help from *him*." However, "It will be no harm to try the old man. He will not eat you, anyway, and something must be done for you."

John went to the farm, which turned out to be quite a large, well-kept place. He found his grandfather "a stern-looking, pink-complexioned, rather stout old gentlemen . . . smoking a long clay pipe."

He told the old man who he was and what he wanted, and when he was finished, the old man took the pipe out of his mouth, pointed the stem toward the door, and said, "Very well. You can go back the same way you came. I can do nothing for you, and have nothing to give you."

Years later the great explorer wrote, "I have forgotten a million of things, probably, but there are some few pictures and some few phrases that one can never forget. The insolent, cold-blooded manner impressed them on my memory, and if I have recalled the scene once, it has been recalled a thousand times." He had no better luck with his maternal uncles, though at least they fed him before sending him on his way.

He was finally taken in by a cousin named Moses Owen, who was a schoolmaster in the village of Brynford. John was to work as sort of a pupil-teacher, but the arrangement was never very satisfactory. John regarded his schoolfellows as louts. "It would be easier to transform apes into men, than to make such natures gentle." When they discovered his workhouse origins, they teased him mercilessly. "The effect was to drive me within my own shell, and to impress the lesson on me that I was forever banned by having been an inmate of the Workhouse."

Moses Owen soon came to regret his burst of generosity to the boy. But instead of coming right out and saying that he could no longer afford to keep John, Moses became more and more irritable. The boy was continually told he was "a blockhead, an idiot." "Your head must be full of mud instead of brains. Seven hours for one proposition! I never knew the equal of this numbskull." After the nine months' term, John left the school and never returned.

He lodged for a while with Moses' mother, Mary Owen, who kept a sort of tavern. This was the Aunt Mary he was supposed to be going to see the day he was taken to the workhouse. She was not a cruel woman, but rather a hard and practical one. She let the boy know that he could stay only a short while, yet the next few months were some of the happiest he had yet experienced. Aunt Mary had always been straightforward with him, and he appreciated that.

Next he was packed off to another aunt in Liverpool—where it was hoped he would find work. John had lived his life either behind the walls of the workhouse or in tiny Welsh villages. Suddenly he found himself in a city. The noise and the crowds amazed and panicked him. But he was greeted joyfully by his Aunt Marie and particularly his Uncle Tom, a hearty, expansive, but impractical man. Tom kept promising to find the boy a good job but was unable to deliver on the promise. In fact, he actually wound up borrowing the small sum that John had saved.

The boy then began tramping the streets looking for work on his own, and he finally found some with a haberdasher, cleaning up, moving stock, and taking down and putting up the heavy shutters that covered the front of the store at night. Work began at seven in the morning and ended at nine at night, six days a week. For this John was paid five shillings—less than a dollar a week. He lasted two months until "the weight of the shutters conquered me, and sent me to bed for a week to recuperate." By the time he got back, the haberdasher had hired a stronger and older boy. John spent the next month tramping through the streets again. He was constantly told that he was too young, too small, or not smart enough for the job.

He finally did find work as an errand boy for a butcher near the docks. The butcher was a brute, and relations with his relatives had deteriorated. John Rowlands was in an "indifferent mood," not knowing what to do with his life when "[f]ate caused a little incident to occur which settled my course for me." He made a delivery to Captain David Hardinge of the American packet ship *Windermere*. As he was staring at the rich furnishings of the captain's cabin, he became aware that the captain was watching him.

"I see," said the captain, "that you admire my cabin. How would you like to live in it?"

John was astonished. He was being asked if he wanted to go to sea. He protested he knew nothing of sailing.

"Sho! You will learn all that you have to do; and in time, you may become a captain of as fine a ship. We skippers have all been boys, you know. Come, what do you say to going with me as cabin-boy? I will give you five dollars a month, and an outfit. In three days we start for New Orleans, to the land of the free and the home of the brave."

John barely hesitated. "I will go with you sir, if you think I will suit."

His aunt and uncle were genuinely unhappy to see him go, but finally they consented. On December 20, 1858, John Rowlands took a steam tug to the *Windermere* and soon discovered something about ocean voyages that he had never known of before—seasickness. For three days he simply lay in the ship's hold "oblivious, helpless and grieving." On the fourth day he found out that he had been betrayed once again.

John thought he had signed on as a cabin boy, but it was really just part of the captain's scheme to get cheap deckhands. He learned that he was to be treated so badly that in New Orleans he would be forced to jump ship, for fear of what might happen on the return voyage, and the captain could then pocket the twenty-five dollars in wages he had accumulated.

This information was passed on to John by a young shipmate named Harry, who told him that the chief tormentor would be Nelson, the second mate. "The second mate is bad enough, but Waters, the chief mate, is the very devil. With him the blow goes before the word, while Nelson roars like a true sea-dog before he strikes. Good Lord, I've seen some sights aboard this packet, I have." Harry, who intended to be a seaman, was immune to such treatment. "My father saw me properly shipped, and I signed articles. . . . The skipper has to account for me when he gets to port; but you, you may be blown overboard, and no one would be the wiser."

John greatly admired the dashing young Harry. "Long Hart, the cook, was another kind of hero to me." The cook was gigantic and wore golden earrings. "During dog-watches he spun long yarns about his experiences in deep-sea ships, and voyages to Callao, California, the West Coast of Africa, and elsewhere, many of which were horrible on account of the cruelty practiced on sailors."

However, John could not easily join in comradeship even with those aboard the *Windermere* whom he admired, primarily because they swore so freely. The rigid morality of the workhouse was always a part of him. Though he traveled all over the world, in the company of all manner of men, swearing always upset him.

John was not the lowest member of the ship's company, because five days out of Liverpool three stowaways were discovered, two Irish boys of about fourteen and fifteen and an Irishman "ragged, haggard, and spiritless from hunger and sickness." Most of Nelson's blows were directed toward the stowaways. The mates were generally brutal toward the crew until the ship neared port, then they quite suddenly changed. "The mates astonished me by their extravagant praise of those they had so cruelly mauled and beaten." The reason, John was told, was that the mates feared that if they made too many enemies they might wind up dead in some New Orleans alleyway.

After a voyage of six weeks the *Windermere* sailed up the Mississippi to New Orleans. John had never experienced anything like the city. "The soft, balmy air, with its strange scents of fermenting molasses, semi-baked sugar, green coffee, pitch, Stockholm tar, brine of mess-beef, rum and whiskey drippings. . . . In some places the freights lay in mountainous heaps, but the barrels, and hogsheads and cotton bales, covered immense spaces . . . with multitudes of men—white, red, black, yellow,—horses, mules, and drays and wagons, the effect of such a scene with its fierce activity and new atmosphere upon a raw boy from St. Asaph, may be better imagined than described."

John followed his friend Harry into the teeming streets. They had dinner at a boardinghouse, and after dinner Harry led him to another sort of house, "the proprietress of which was extremely gracious." His workhouse upbringing had left John Rowlands profoundly ignorant about sex, and when four scantily clad young ladies entered the room "and proceeded to take liberties with my person," he fled in horror.

Harry followed and tried to persuade his inexperienced friend to have a drink, but John insisted that he had signed a pledge never to drink. "Well, smoke then, do something like other fellows," exclaimed the exasperated Harry. John had never heard that smoking was a moral offense, so he lit up a cigar and promptly got sick. "Thus ended my first night at New Orleans."

When John got back to the ship, he found Nelson waiting for him. The second mate was surprised and not at all happy to see the boy, and he set to work making sure that John would run away without collecting the wages he was owed. After five days of merciless badgering, John couldn't stand it anymore. He packed his best shore clothes and the bishop's Bible and ran from the *Windermere*, cutting his ties with England.

Without any money, he knew he had to find some sort of work or starve. He saw a kindly-looking middle-aged man wearing a dark suit and tall hat sitting in front of a door in the custom house. Taking the man to be the proprietor of one of the stores, John approached him and asked cautiously if he needed someone to help with the work in the store.

Once again John Rowlands's life was about to take a dramatic and unexpected turn.

CHAPTER 3

America

The man in the dark suit and tall hat whom young John Rowlands approached was a prosperous traveling merchant by the name of Henry Morton Stanley. Stanley had been happily married for many years, but the one great disappointment in his life was that he had no children to succeed him in his business. For that reason he did not immediately dismiss the awkward-looking and obviously foreign eighteen-year-old who had approached him, though he had no need of any sort of employee.

He questioned John about where he had come from and why he was looking for work. John told him briefly of his experiences aboard the *Windermere*.

"So," said the gentleman, "you are friendless in a strange land, eh, and want work to begin making your fortune, eh? Well, what work can you do? Can you read? What book is that in your pocket?"

It was the bishop's Bible, and Stanley was impressed

by the inscription. Before going into business, Stanley had been a preacher, and he remained a very religious man. He then had John read an article from the newspaper, which he said was delivered "very correctly, but with an un-American accent."

Then he had John mark some coffee sacks with an *S* and the words *MEMPHIS, TENN.* When he was finished, Stanley cried, "Excellent! Even better than I could do it myself. There is no chance of my coffee getting lost this time! Well, I must see what can be done for you."

The first order of business was to take John to breakfast; the next was to get him a haircut. He was then brought back to the store where he had first approached Stanley, and introduced to the owner, a Mr. James Speake. On Stanley's recommendation, Speake took the boy on for a week's trial. Stanley then left saying, "I am going up-river with my consignments, but I shall return shortly and hope to hear the best accounts of you."

John Rowlands blossomed in his new life in a new country. He was such a diligent worker that he was not only given a permanent position but his salary was raised. He rented a room in a boardinghouse run by a Mrs. Williams, who treated him with "maternal solicitude." For the first time in his life he had some extra cash, and since he had none of the ordinary vices upon which young men spend their money, John invested his in books. His first purchase was Gibbon's *Decline and Fall of the Roman Empire.* He bought it because he had heard of it when he was in the workhouse. There were also books like Spenser's *Faerie Queene* and Plutarch's *Lives,* and a large *History of the United States,* "which I sadly needed, because of my utter ignorance of the country I was in."

The United States was not the only thing about

which John Rowlands was utterly ignorant. One day another boy appeared at Mrs. Williams's boardinghouse. Like John he had come from Liverpool aboard a ship where he was treated brutally, and for that reason he had jumped ship the moment he touched port. Since the boardinghouse was full, Mrs. Williams asked John if the new boy, Dick Heaton, could share his room. Since they seemed to have shared similar experiences John readily agreed.

Dick seemed a clever and cheerful lad, and the two soon became friends. But John's new roommate had some peculiar ways. There was only one bed in the room, a large four-poster. But Dick always lay on the far edge of the bed; moreover, he never undressed before going to bed. He told John that on shipboard he got into the habit of sleeping with his clothes on because he had once been beaten severely for dressing too slowly. He also said that he padded his clothes to fortify himself against the blows. Still, padding did not entirely explain his "unusual forward inclination of the body, and singular leanness of the shoulders." When John said to him that he walked more like a girl than a boy, Dick retorted, "So do you." They both had a good laugh over the remark.

One morning John awoke, and he noticed that Dick's shirt was open at the neck. On his chest he saw what he took to be two tumors. His gasp of surprise awakened his companion. "He asked what was the matter? Pointing to his open breast, I anxiously inquired if those were not painful?"

John was told pointedly to mind his own business. As he sat there feeling rather irritated, he began to put together the observations of the last few days, and as he later described it, suddenly "I sat up triumphantly, and cried out with the delight of a discoverer:—

"'I know! I know! Dick, you are a girl!'"

When "Dick" looked at him and coolly admitted to the accusation, John became so frightened that he jumped out of bed "as though I had been scorched!"

Dick Heaton turned out to be Alice Heaton. According to Alice, she had escaped from the home of her grandmother, who hated her and whom she hated in return. She had managed to ship out on the American brig the *Pocahontas* disguised as a boy, and somehow she had escaped discovery. After hearing this amazing story, John had to rush off to work, and when he returned, Alice was gone. He never saw or heard of her again. Though he admired her "artful and bold character" and her "uncommon spirit," he decided that fate was "wise in separating two young and simple creatures, who might have been led, through excess of sentiment, into folly."

Henry Stanley's business trip had kept him away from New Orleans for about a month. When he returned, he was delighted to find his young protégé getting on so well. John was invited for Sunday breakfast to the imposing Stanley home on St. Charles Street. Mrs. Stanley, "a fragile little lady, who was the picture of refinement," awed the boy. She was, he said, "the first lady I ever conversed with." Mrs. Stanley took a liking to the unsophisticated and quiet lad, and John Rowlands became a regular visitor at the Stanley house.

At work, matters did not proceed so well. During the summer of 1859 New Orleans was suffering through one of its regular epidemics of yellow fever. Mr. Speake caught the disease and died. The business was sold to a man named Ellison, who was a good deal less sympathetic to young John. Mrs. Stanley also fell ill, and since Henry Stanley was away, John asked his new employer for a few days leave to help take care of the sick woman. This was refused, and John quit on the spot.

John hung around the Stanley house, in a state of desperate anxiety about Mrs. Stanley's health. But there was nothing that he or anyone else could do. She died in a few days. The day after her death Henry Stanley's brother, a ship captain from Havana, arrived and took charge of everything. John, feeling miserable and unwanted, withdrew.

He went in search of another job but was unable to find anything better than temporary work. His best job was attendant for a sick sea captain. This lasted for about four weeks, and John and the captain, a patient and pious soul, became fast friends. Before he left, the captain gave him more than his promised wages as a "token of regard" and advised him to seek his friend (Stanley) in St. Louis. John immediately booked passage on a steamer sailing up the river to St. Louis. When he reached St. Louis and inquired at the Planters Hotel, where he knew Stanley usually stayed, he found that the merchant had checked out and gone back to New Orleans.

John now looked, unsuccessfully, for work in St. Louis. He finally got a job on a flatboat that was going back to New Orleans. His voyage as a crewman on a riverboat was a much more agreeable experience than was his first sea voyage. The flatboat men were a boisterous but good-natured lot who didn't swear nearly as much as the sailors of the *Windermere*. The trip was really a rather lazy one, and John had plenty of time to study river navigation, though it was far from apparent at the time that the knowledge he gained would one day be very useful to him.

As soon as he reached New Orleans, John Rowlands hurried to the Stanley house on St. Charles Street, the place where he had found the closest thing to a real family that he had ever known. His meeting with Henry

Stanley was an emotional one. The merchant had heard of John's concern and helpfulness during his wife's illness, and he told the boy that he would take charge of his future. John Rowlands, who had not cried since his early days in the workhouse, broke down sobbing. "It was the only tender action I had ever known, and, what no amount of cruelty could have forced from me, tears poured in a torrent. . . ."

The merchant wanted the outcast boy to be the son he had never had. He had only one requirement, "in future you are to bear my name, Henry Stanley." The merchant then dipped his hand in a basin of water and made the sign of the cross on the boy's forehead. For some reason Henry Stanley never actually legally adopted the boy. Still, as far as the former John Rowlands was concerned, this was the father he had never had, and more. For the next two years the merchant and the boy traveled up and down the Mississippi on business. This period Henry Stanley—for that is what he can properly be called now—regarded as the happiest in his life. None of the great accomplishments of his later years ever overshadowed the time he spent with the man he called his father.

Young Stanley possessed a remarkable memory. He could recall names, faces, prices, and the destinations of shipments with unfailing accuracy—a great advantage for a traveling merchant. The elder Stanley also continued his protégé's education. Whenever they would stop at a large city, they would buy books of all types— no light novels or romances, however, for the merchant held rigid views on literature. He also had rigid views about drinking and gambling and warned the boy against the evils of the steamer saloons with their gambling halls, which were common sights on the river. These views fitted perfectly with the younger Stanley's stern work-house morality. They made an odd and austere pair on the colorful pre–Civil War Mississippi, with its riverboat gamblers and easy morals.

The Stanleys could not entirely cut themselves off from the restless and often violent life of the river. Once in mid-1860 the Stanleys were traveling on the steamer *Little Rock*, and the merchant was carrying a great deal of money. In the evening young Stanley saw a man listening at his father's cabin door. The stranger then quietly entered the room. Henry heard noises, rushed in, and found the stranger wrestling with his father. When the intruder saw the young man he pulled a knife, but he only cut the boy's coat. The intruder fled but was never captured.

A few months after this incident, the elder Stanley heard that his sea captain brother in Havana was ill. He also thought it was time to find a more settled business for his adopted son. He planned to go to Havana and made arrangements for Henry to work as a clerk in a backwoods store at Cypress Bend, Arkansas—a part of the South that the merchant thought had great promise for future development. He also met a Major Ingham, an old friend who invited the boy to spend some time on his plantation in Saline County, Arkansas.

Henry was enthusiastic about the plans, at first. But when the moment came for the elder Stanley to leave, Henry was devastated. Years later he wrote, "I have not experienced such wretchedness as I did that night following his departure." Life had made young Henry Stanley wary of emotional commitments, but once he made a commitment it was deep and permanent.

Major Ingham took young Stanley to his plantation— really just a large log house—deep in the Arkansas pine forest. He was welcomed by the Ingham family. There was, however, one sour note, a rather oafish and brutal overseer. "I set him down at once as one of those men who haunt liquor-saloons, and are proud to claim the acquaintance with bar-tenders." The overseer also took an immediate dislike to young Stanley.

One day Stanley was helping the major's black slaves cut down pine trees. It was the sort of physical labor that he loved. The overseer was in an exceptionally bad humor.

"A young fellow named Jim was the first victim of his ire, and, as he was carrying a heavy log with myself and others, he could not answer him so politely as he expected. He flicked at his naked shoulders with his whip, and the lash flying unexpectedly near me caused us both to drop our spikes." The other men were unable to hold the log, and it fell, crushing one man's foot.

Stanley had seen and experienced much brutality in his short life and was not at all tenderhearted. But the overseer seemed to him a combination of Simon Legree from *Uncle Tom's Cabin* and Nelson, the bullying second mate of the *Windermere*. There was an argument, and Stanley and the overseer almost came to blows. Stanley complained to Major Ingham, who only smiled politely and said that that was the way things were done on the plantation. Stanley packed his bags and left immediately. A few days later he arrived at Mr. Altschul's store at Cypress Bend, where he was to serve as a clerk.

It was a swampy, unhealthful climate, and like everyone else in the area, Henry came down with "Arkansas ague"—probably malaria. He had severe fever attacks on the average of three times a month. Stanley always claimed the Arkansas disease was worse then any similar disease he encountered in Africa. During the worst attacks his once-chubby body was reduced to skeletal thinness.

The store was located in a primitive area. The richer folk lived on plantations of six to ten square miles and owned hundreds of slaves. Stanley observed, "They lived like princelings." They were a prickly lot, quick to defend any insult, real or imagined, with a duel. In fact, dueling or just shooting one another was common in that region. "Every new immigrant soon became infected with the proud and sensitive spirit prevailing in Arkansas. The poor American settler, the Irish employee, the German-Jew storekeeper in a brief time grew as liable to bursts of deadly passion or fits of cold-blooded malignity, as the Virginian aristocrat." Though Stanley himself never actually engaged in a duel or shot anyone, he did a lot of target shooting and became very proficient with a pistol.

While in Arkansas, Stanley received three letters from his "father" in Havana. The last one said that his brother was recovering, and that he would soon return to New Orleans and then come up to Arkansas to pay his son a visit. Henry Stanley the elder never returned; he died in Havana in 1861. The younger Stanley waited for a visit that never came. In fact, he did not even hear about his father's death for years, because he was overwhelmed by events that he barely understood.

A Welshman by birth, Stanley had no natural interest in American politics. He rarely read newspapers, so he didn't know much about the election of Abraham Lincoln and the sentiment in the South to secede from the Union. When Stanley first became aware of the possibility of war, he worried only about how it would affect business and how a war might prevent his father from traveling up the Mississippi. All those around him were ready, even anxious for war—"war mad," Stanley called them. They all seemed convinced that the Yankees would be easily defeated.

The young men of Stanley's age rushed to join the "Dixie Grays," a local regiment. "It seemed as if Arkansas County was to be emptied of all the youth and men I had known." Yet Stanley held back—it was not his war. Then one day he received an anonymous package containing a bundle of lady's underwear—the package carried with it the charge of cowardice. That afternoon the local recruiter for the Dixie Grays appeared and asked Stanley if he was ready to "join the valiant children of Arkansas to fight." The thoroughly humiliated Stanley answered, "Yes."

So the rather innocent and puzzled Stanley became a member of the Confederate army. For a while it was exhilarating. The former workhouse boy rubbed shoulders with the sons of some of the South's oldest and richest families. He was swept away by the enthusiasm of war and became "fluent in the jargon of patriotism." Everywhere the Dixie Grays went they were cheered, and Stanley joined the others in singing "We'll live and die for Dixie." Of course, no one really thought of dying, for none of the eager young soldiers had ever been in a battle, and all were convinced that one Southerner could easily lick ten cowardly Yankees.

The first long march destroyed a lot of illusions. By nightfall the smartly dressed, quick-stepping regiment had been reduced to a rabble of exhausted, limping stragglers. War was not going to be as easy as everyone had assumed. Conditions grew steadily worse, for there was a continual shortage of food, and the soldiers were forced to steal from reputed "antisecessionists." As discipline began to break down, punishment became correspondingly severe. Even a small offense might result in the culprit's being hoisted up by his thumbs or being painfully tied and gagged.

Privately, Stanley was beginning to have grave doubts about the wisdom of having joined up—and he had still not yet seen any fighting. For nine months the regiment had been shifted around the South. On April 4, 1862, the Dixie Grays were marched out of Corinth, Mississippi, to join forces with Generals Albert Sidney Johnson and Pierre Beauregard, who planned to surprise the army of Ulysses Grant, which was encamped at the Tennessee River near Shiloh. It turned out to be one of the bloodiest battles of the entire Civil War.

As with most common soldiers in a battle, Stanley had little knowledge of what was actually happening. Early on the morning of April 6, 1862, Stanley's regiment formed part of a three-mile line that was to drive the Union troops back to the Tennessee River. As soldiers advanced, they heard firing in the distance; then bullets began whizzing through the trees above their heads. "We are in for it now," said the man next to Stanley. They continued to advance, and the captain shouted, "There they are!" and "Aim low, men!" Stanley began firing, though he at first couldn't see what he was firing at. Finally he caught sight of "a long line of bluey figures." As Stanley and his fellow soldiers took a step forward, the blue figures seemed to take a step back.

Then came the order "Fix bayonets! On the double quick!" That order triggered a fierce yell from the Southern line. "It drove all sanity and order from among us." The savage yells and the sight of thousands of charging troops seemed to break the spirit of the Union forces, which turned and ran, abandoning their camp. Stanley and the others, who had been caught up in sort of a rapturous fury, rushed into the camp, believing that the battle was over. In truth it had just begun, for right behind the camp they captured was another camp, and behind that another and another. The Union forces outnumbered the Confederates. The firing became more intense, and progress was much slower. The soldiers were forced to take cover on the ground behind some fallen logs. For the first time Stanley saw that the men around him were being killed.

"One man raised his chest, as if to yawn, and jostled me. I turned to him, and saw that a bullet had gored his whole face, and penetrated his chest. Another ball struck a man a deadly rap on the head, and he turned on his back and showed his ghastly white face to the sky." By ten o'clock Stanley was totally exhausted, when something struck him on the belt buckle and knocked him to the ground. The buckle probably saved his life—and he just lay on the earth for a while, thankful to be alive and for the chance to rest.

He had become separated from his company, and in his attempt to catch up with them, he passed one scene of horrors after the other. One that especially stuck in his mind was a half-mile square of wood, "lighted brightly by the sun, and littered by the forms of about a thousand dead and wounded men, and by horses, and military equipments."

At about one o'clock Stanley caught up with the Dixie Grays. They were still pushing the Union troops slowly backward, but their numbers had been thinned considerably, and they were now under fire from Union gunboats on the river. Late in the afternoon they captured another Union camp and were allowed to retire for the night. Stanley found some biscuits and a canteen of molasses, stuffed himself, crawled into one of the tents, and fell asleep. It rained that night but he was not disturbed.

Stanley awoke before dawn the next morning feeling refreshed, under the mistaken impression that a great victory had been won. As the Dixies lined up, Stanley realized that there were only about fifty of them left, and some of them were wounded or otherwise in poor condition for a prolonged battle. Now the Union troops were advancing. The Dixies were to go out to meet them. As the men were lining up, Stanley's company commander called out, "Now, Mr. Stanley, if you please, step briskly forward!" Stanley was stung by being singled out in that way, and he stepped forward more quickly than he should have. He suddenly found himself in an open field with the Union troops moving in on him. He jumped into a hollow and assumed that the rest of his company was right behind him. They weren't—he was all alone. The next thing he heard was, "Down with that gun, Secesh, or I'll drill a hole through you! Drop it quick!" Half a dozen Union soldiers were pointing their guns at him. As he dropped his own, two of them rushed forward and grabbed him. Henry Stanley was a prisoner.

As Stanley, the prisoner, was marched through enemy lines, some soldiers shouted curses at him and threatened him with their bayonets, but his guards protected him. Stanley worried about the shame of being captured and about the loss of his knapsack, "and my little treasures,—letters, and souvenirs of my father? They were lost beyond recovery!"

That very day Stanley and a group of equally miserable-looking Confederate prisoners were loaded aboard a steamer and taken to St. Louis, where they were penned up for a few days in what had once been a girls' school.

They were then packed into railroad cars and taken to a prisoner-of-war compound, Camp Douglas, on the outskirts of Chicago.

"Our prison-pen was a square and spacious enclosure, like a bleak cattle-yard, walled high with planking, on the top of which, at every sixty yards or so, were sentry boxes. About fifty feet from its base, and running parallel with it, was a line of lime wash. That was the 'deadline,' and any prisoner who crossed it was liable to be shot."

About three thousand men were housed in twenty barnlike structures. They slept on hay piled on wooden platforms. Each man had a single blanket. Stanley admitted that the prisoners were not abused physically and that the food was passable. But the sanitary and medical facilities at Camp Douglas were horrendous. The latrines were open ditches with a stench so powerful that many men already weakened by confinement collapsed at the edge and lay there for hours, unable to move. "Exhumed corpses could not have presented any thing more hideous than dozens of these dead-and-alive men, who, oblivious to the weather, hung over the latrines, or lay extended along the open sewer. . . . "

Naturally diseases such as dysentery and typhus raged under such conditions. Every day wagonloads of corpses were carried out of the camp.

Inside the barracks vermin multiplied. Even the piles of dust on the floor moved. And there was nothing to do aside from a few simple housekeeping tasks. The prisoners were not given a book or newspaper to read, there were no visitors—nothing. The tedium as much as anything else broke their spirit. "We were soon in a fair state of rotting, while yet alive." Men sat blankly staring at the wall.

Stanley was put in charge of handling the food for his barracks, and he struck up a friendship with a Mr. Shipman, who was in charge of the commissary. Shipman told the young prisoner that there was only one way to get out of Camp Douglas and that was to desert the Confederate cause and join the Union army. Stanley was at first shocked by the suggestion. Shipman continued to work on him. As a foreigner Stanley had no deep commitment to the South, yet all the Americans he knew, including his adopted father, were Southerners. He didn't know anything about politics, and at that moment in his life, he saw nothing wrong with slavery.

Shipman had a more powerful argument. "They have taken two wagon-loads of dead men away this morning," he said. Stanley feared dying in prison, or worse still, remaining half alive in the hellhole for years. After about six weeks in Camp Douglas, Henry Stanley agreed to enroll in the Union army, and on June 4 he was released from Camp Douglas. His career as a Union soldier lasted three days. He was shipped to Harpers Ferry, Virginia; then dysentery and some unknown fever that he had also contracted in prison struck. Stanley was sent to the hospital and stayed there until June 22, when he was discharged, "a wreck."

At that moment Henry Stanley's condition was just about as bleak as it could possibly be. He was penniless, friendless, sick, and he had no idea where to go. All he possessed in the world were a pair of blue militia trousers, a dark coat, and a "mongrel hat." Stanley started walking from Harpers Ferry to Hagerstown—a distance of some twenty-four miles. He could not walk three hundred yards without gasping for breath; he was feverish and bleeding internally. It took him a week to cover half the distance. The filthy, feverish Stanley begged permission from a farmer to sleep in his corn silo. He woke up several days later in a bed in the farmhouse. He had been washed and given a clean shirt. The farmer took care of him, and with good food and fresh air Stanley recovered quickly enough to be able to help with the harvest in July. Stanley stayed with the farmer for another month. Then his benefactor drove him to the railway station and gave him fare to Baltimore. Once again Henry Stanley had dodged the bullet.

He managed to get a variety of jobs and saved enough money for passage back to Liverpool, for he felt he no longer had a place in war-torn America. He made his way to Denbigh, the town in which he was born, and to his mother's house. Stanley was still subject to recurring attacks of fever, he had no money, and he was dressed shabbily, yet he wanted to show his mother that he had grown up, that he had become a man. Perhaps he would finally be able to find a home.

His mother took one look at the ragged, sickly figure and told him that he was a disgrace in the eyes of the neighbors and that he should leave as quickly as possible. This rejection left an even deeper impression on Stanley than his original abandonment.

Since his natural family had thrown him out, Stanley returned once again to America to search for his adopted father. He journeyed to Cuba only to discover that the elder Stanley had died there nearly two years earlier.

Stanley was crushed, and at this point he appears to have given up the idea of seeking a life of comfort, security, and family warmth. His hopes had been dashed too many times. If he was meant to be a loner and a wanderer, then so be it. He once again turned to the sea, and throughout 1863 and early 1864 he sailed to the West Indies, Spain, and Italy. He kept an incomplete diary for this period, and sometimes the most exciting events were condensed into brief entries:

"Wrecked off Barcelona. Crew lost in night. Stripped naked, and swam to shore. Barrack of Carbineers . . . demanded my papers."

Even on shore he could not escape danger and rejection. A late 1863 entry contains these words about a place he was staying in Brooklyn, New York:

"Boarding with Judge X——. Judge drunk; tried to kill his wife with hatchet; attempted three times.—I held him down all night. Next morning, exhausted; lighted cigar in parlour; wife came down—insulted and raved at me for smoking in her house!"

In August 1864 Stanley enlisted in the U.S. Navy. He attained the rating of ship's writer—it was his duty to keep the log and the other ship's records. Though the war was finally ending, there was still much to record, including two dramatic and bloody attacks on Fort Fisher, North Carolina, the Confederacy's last open port.

It was as ship's writer that Stanley apparently first got the idea of making a living as a journalist. He sent his firsthand accounts of the attacks to some newspapers, and they were printed. Henry Stanley finally found the profession that was to make him famous.

CHAPTER 4

The Reporter

By 1865 the Civil War was winding down, and service in an inactive navy could not satisfy Stanley's restless nature. In February 1865, Stanley along with a young shipmate named Louis Noe simply walked away from the *Minnesota*, on which they had been serving. Stanley may have been the only man to serve in the Confederate army, the Union army, and the Union navy.

The war ended two months after Stanley's desertion, and by that time he was working as a journalist, first in New York, then as a free-lance reporter throughout the West. His sketchy diary records such names as "St. Joseph, Missouri—across the Plains—Indians,—Salt Lake City,—Denver,—Black Hawk,—Omaha." He floated down the Platte River on a flat-bottomed boat. There are few details of his life from this period, except in Omaha.

There Stanley fell in with a theatrical troupe. Apparently he arranged some sort of benefit for them. Afterward there was a party at which Stanley forgot his nondrinking pledge and got roaring drunk. At first everything was hilarious, all his companions wonderful friends, all the women were beautiful. According to his diary, at about two o'clock in the morning, "We sallied out, singing, 'We won't go home till morning.' . . . I wonder now we were not shot at. . . ." The following morning Stanley awoke with a ferocious hangover and an overpowering feeling of remorse. He swore that he would never get drunk again, and he never did.

At this point Stanley, along with a traveling companion named W. H. Cook and Stanley's fellow deserter from the Navy, Louis Noe, got the idea of going to the Orient. They put together the money (mostly Cook's) for an expedition to Turkey and set sail from Boston to Smyrna on July 11, 1866. It was an ill-fated venture. On their first night in the Turkish countryside Noe decided to play a joke on Cook by setting a small fire. The fire got out of hand and destroyed a large area of vineyards. The local villagers were enraged, and Stanley managed to calm them only with great difficulty. Six days later a treacherous guide led them to the camp of a band of Turkoman robbers who beat, robbed, and threatened to kill them. The robbers spared the lives of the three travelers, in hope of getting a ransom for them. They were taken to the nearest village and thrown into a "semi-civilized prison."

Then their luck changed, for their plight came to the attention of an agent of the Imperial Ottoman Bank, who managed to secure the release of the three Americans and have the real bandits thrown into prison. The trio was also befriended by Edward Joy Morris, the American minister at Constantinople, who gave them £150. In exchange Stanley gave Morris a worthless check, but he was desperate. Wisely Morris did not try to cash the check, and ultimately he got his money back from the Turkish government. Stanley made a little on the adventure by writing it up for an English-language newspaper in Turkey.

Stanley then made one more try at reconciling himself with his family. He appeared in Denbigh wearing a U.S. Navy uniform and putting out the story that he was still in the navy. He also signed himself John Rowlands, perhaps for the last time in his life. His mother wasn't exactly overjoyed to see him, but at least he now looked clean and didn't ask for anything, so he was allowed to stay for a few days. He also paid a visit to the St. Asaph workhouse (the sadistic Francis was long gone). At the workhouse he posed as a successful "graduate," buying tea and cakes for the boys and lecturing them on the virtues and rewards of hard work.

In March 1867 Stanley was back in the United States, where he got a job as special correspondent for the Missouri *Democrat*. Stanley was to accompany a large military expedition led by General Winfield Scott Hancock into Indian country.

The years following the Civil War saw an enormous push westward by prospective settlers. A rail line spanning the continent was being constructed at the rate of four miles a day, and new wagon roads were constantly being cut through territory that had once been the sole domain of the Indians. These Native American peoples resisted the inroads with sporadic uprisings. It was Hancock's job to placate those tribes that could be placated, but, if necessary, to subdue those that could not. This was the expedition that Stanley was to report on.

On his way West the young journalist stopped off in St. Louis, where he met Mark Twain and Joseph Pulitzer, both of whom were also working as journalists at the time. But it was Stanley who traveled with the army and left the most complete record available of this important period of American history. Historian Dee Brown wrote, "Certainly no one equaled Stanley in his reportage of that exciting time when rails were first being laid across the Great Plains, the stage was being set for the Indian wars in the West, and the first trail-driving cowboys were herding longhorns north from Texas. Without Stanley's descriptions of these events, we would lack some of the most spirited images of that colorful episode in our history."

Stanley met General George Armstrong Custer. "A certain impetuosity and undoubted courage are his principal characteristics," he wrote.

One of the men attached to the army was James Butler "Wild Bill" Hickok, who might best be described as a gentleman killer. "I say, Mr. Hickok, how many white men have you killed to your certain knowledge?" asked Stanley. Hickok was well known for his hatred of Indians, and barely considered killing an Indian even worth mentioning.

Hickok thought for a moment and replied, "I suppose I have killed considerably over a hundred."

"What made you kill all those men? Did you kill them without cause or provocation?"

"No by heaven! I never killed one man without good cause."

"How old were you when you killed your first white man, and for what cause?"

"I was twenty-eight years old when I killed the first white man, and if ever a man deserved killing he did. He was a gambler and counterfeiter. . . ."

Stanley found Wild Bill remarkably cultured, charming, and well spoken. "He is more inclined to be sociable than otherwise."

When he began writing about his adventures in Africa, Stanley was often criticized as being a humorless writer. But his dispatches from the Great Plains display a good grasp of frontier humor. Upon entering a little town in Kansas he wrote:

"The population of the town of Ellsworth is estimated at forty men, four women, eight boys and seven girls. There are also fourteen horses, and about twenty-nine and one-half dogs. . . . As Ellsworth is part and parcel of this great and prosperous country, it is also progressive—for no sooner has the fifth house begun to erect its stately front above the green earth, than the population is gathered in the three saloons to gravely discuss the propriety of making the new town a city, and electing a mayor." A young Mark Twain could not have done better.

The bulk of Stanley's reports were about the Indians. Though he titillated his readers with tales of massacres, scalpings, and other outrages, none of which he personally observed, he also displayed considerable sympathy toward the Native Americans, whose lands and way of life were being destroyed by the encroachments of settlers and the railroads. "Few can read the speeches of the Indian chiefs without feeling deep sympathy for them; they move us by their pathos and mournful dignity." Stanley quoted with approval the statement of General Harney: "The Indians are a great deal better than we are."

Despite his sympathy, Stanley was completely on the side of the whites' civilization and was convinced that the Indians and their way of life were doomed. "They were asking the impossible. The half of a continent could not be kept as a buffalo pasture and hunting ground." Stanley had been sent to the West to cover the Indian wars, but he didn't see a single battle. He did, however, observe a large number of conferences with the Indians, and he felt that he learned a lot about dealing with tribal peoples, a knowledge he was to put to good use later in Africa. He said that in Central Africa he repeated almost verbatim a speech made by General William Tecumseh Sherman to the Sioux on the Great Plains.

In December of 1867 Stanley was back in New York looking for more journalistic work. His reports on the Indian campaign had gained him enough fame to secure an interview with James Gordon Bennett, Jr., the eccentric and brilliant young publisher of the New York *Herald*, the largest circulation newspaper in the world. Stanley proposed that the *Herald* send him to Africa to cover the British campaign in Abyssinia (present-day Ethiopia). Bennett didn't think the campaign held sufficient interest for American readers to justify the expense of a regular correspondent. However, if Stanley wished to go as a "special correspondent," that is, to pay his own way, the *Herald* would be willing to buy his reports if they were "up to the standard," Bennett said. Two days later Stanley was on a boat bound for London, and from there to Africa.

The Abyssinian campaign that Stanley was to report on was a strange affair. The ruler of Abyssinia was King Theodore. He had been the son of a minor chief, had usurped the throne, and had tried to bring a measure of stability to a chaotic land. Theodore made real efforts to abolish the slave trade and reform taxation and the army, and he tried to bring his isolated nation into closer contact with the outside world. But King Theodore was basically too unstable a character to undertake such an enormous job successfully, and the ultimate result was disaster.

The British consul in Abyssinia had urged King Theodore to write a letter to Queen Victoria requesting a treaty with London. This letter was simply ignored by the British Foreign Office, an act which enraged Theodore. In retaliation he imprisoned the consul, the missionaries, and every other British subject he could lay his hands on. That act did get the attention of the British Foreign Office, and for the next several years London tried in a rather blundering way to deal with the increasingly irrational Abyssinian king. Finally the British government decided that the only way to get the prisoners released was to invade Abyssinia. In January 1868, an expeditionary force of 12,000 men under Sir Robert Napier was sent from India to Abyssinia, an enormous and difficult undertaking.

Napier's army was already marching inland to attack Theodore's stronghold at Magdala when Stanley arrived in Africa. With only a buffalo robe from his Western days to shield him from the weather, Stanley hurried after them. "The column," Stanley wrote, "in spite of its martial air, had something of a piebald look." There were English and Irish regiments with their red coats; there were regiments of Punjabis and Baluchis with red fezzes or green turbans; there was a brigade of English sailors; there were horses, camels, elephants, and thousands of mules, and Stanley noticed one aristocratic young officer wearing kid gloves and a green veil.

Henry Stanley with his buffalo robe and the broad American accent he had picked up was something of a curiosity himself—a character out of a novel of the Wild West. The high-born British officers were cold and reserved; they barely spoke to him. Stanley was hurt. The other correspondents, who were mainly from British papers, didn't much like Americans, particularly employees of the notorious New York *Herald*. Yet on the whole Stanley seems to have enjoyed the Abyssinian campaign and ultimately made friends with many of the other reporters, whom he described as "lovable and good tempered." He also wrote enthusiastically of his friendship with a half-mad character nicknamed Captain Smelfungus, who had once been wounded in the head and had never fully recovered his senses. Smelfungus was the only British officer who really helped Stanley.

The campaign, which was supposed to have ended with the release of the British prisoners after an assault on King Theodore's hilltop stronghold of Magdala, was something of an anticlimax. Theodore's army was no match at all for the well-armed British force and was easily routed at every turn. Theodore released the British prisoners unharmed, but to Stanley the captives seemed strangely unenthusiastic about being freed. By the time of the final assault on Magdala, Theodore had completely lost control of the situation. The British swarmed up the hill practically without opposition. Theodore shot himself with a pistol that had once been a present from Queen Victoria. Stanley was reported to have been seen running down the hill waving a bloody rag and claiming it was King Theodore's shirt.

Stanley exaggerated and dubbed the campaign a "modern Crusade . . . among the most wonderfully successful campaigns ever conducted in history." Stanley showed great initiative in getting his story smuggled out of Africa in spite of British army censorship. The world first learned the details of the Abyssinian campaign from Stanley's reports. That was the sort of scoop that Bennett loved, and Stanley was immediately made a permanent member of the *Herald* staff at a salary of two thousand dollars a year. The former workhouse boy had come a long way.

Stanley's next assignment was to go to the island of Crete off the coast of Greece, where a rebellion was simmering. He was staying briefly on the island of Syros near Crete, when he met a Greek girl and impetuously decided to marry her. Her family, however, was cautious—they barely knew him—and asked for a brief wait before the wedding. Stanley agreed and, while waiting, got cold feet and took off for an assignment in Turkey.

In the next two months his diary is filled with names like Smyrna, Rhodes, Athens, Beirut, and Alexandria. He went to Spain to report on a rebellion and then back to London, where he had a brief infatuation with a young Welsh girl from his hometown, but her parents snubbed him.

Despite his success as a journalist, Stanley felt he was continually being snubbed and insulted, particularly by English people. While traveling in Egypt he met a couple of young Englishmen on the train. Since they were newcomers, Stanley took great pains to share his water and food with them, and he explained to them the historical significance of the scenes they were passing. They seemed to be extremely friendly. In Suez they all went to the same hotel, and there Stanley overheard the two Englishmen talking about him. "Had I been a leper or a pariah, I could not have been more slanderously abused." Such experiences burned in Stanley's mind.

In October 1869 Stanley was back in Spain covering the ongoing rebellion. He had just returned to Madrid from "the carnage at Valencia" when he received a telegram that read "Come to Paris on important business." It was signed "Jas. Gordon Bennett, jun."

James Gordon Bennett, Junior, was about to send Henry Morton Stanley on the most extraordinary assignment in journalistic history. Both men were twenty-eight at the time—but there the resemblance ended. Stanley had been brought up in the workhouse. Bennett was the son of a self-made millionaire newspaper publisher and grew up indulged and surrounded by fabulous wealth. Stanley was short, chunky, and red-faced; Bennett, tall and lean with a long face and dark hair. Where Stanley was basically shy and sensitive, Bennett was arrogant and disdainful of all who were poorer than he, and that was practically everyone. He was rude, insensitive, tyrannical, and violently jealous of anyone who appeared to threaten his power and position. Stanley got drunk once in his life. Bennett got drunk regularly and acted bizarrely. He would pick fights with strangers in bars and drive his coach madly through the streets of Paris at midnight, throwing off his clothes as he went. It cost a lot of money to hush up the scandals that surrounded Bennett, but he had a lot of money.

Yet, for all his eccentricities, which would have been considered madness in poorer folk, James Gordon Bennett, Jr., was no mere shadow of his successful father— he was a newspaper man of genius, who set the standard for mass circulation newspapers for thirty years. His paper the New York *Herald* was denounced as a sensational and gossipmongering rag, which it certainly was. But no one could argue with the *Herald*'s success. The most successful single act in Bennett's journalistic career was to send Henry Stanley on a seemingly impossible mission.

Stanley arrived in Paris in the middle of the night and went straight to Bennett's rooms at the Grand Hotel. Bennett was in bed when Stanley entered.

"Who are you?" Bennett snapped.

"My name is Stanley!"

"Ah, yes! Sit down; I have important business on hand for you."

Bennett put on a robe and asked, "Where do you think Livingstone is?" This was a reference to the celebrated Scottish missionary David Livingstone, who had been exploring in Central Africa but had not been heard from for over a year.

Stanley knew very little about Livingstone and said so.

"Do you think he is alive?" Bennett persisted.

"He may be, and he may not be!"

"Well, I think he is alive, and that he can be found, and I am going to send you to find him."

"What!" Stanley exclaimed. "Do you really think I can find Dr. Livingstone? Do you mean me to go to Central Africa?"

That was exactly what Bennett meant. He told Stanley he could get whatever help he required. "Act according to your own plans, and do what you think best—BUT FIND LIVINGSTONE!"

Stanley was cautious. Bennett was known to be a man of sudden enthusiasms and abrupt changes of heart. More than one *Herald* reporter had been left stranded in a remote land when the impetuous Bennett lost interest in a project. Stanley pointed out that an expedition to Central Africa was likely to cost a great deal of money.

"Well, I will tell you what you will do. Draw a thousand pounds now; and when you have gone through that, draw another thousand, and when that is spent, draw another thousand, and when you have finished that, draw another thousand, and so on; but FIND LIVINGSTONE!"

Stanley was dumbfounded. "Do you mean me to go straight to Africa to search for Dr. Livingstone?"

"No! I wish you to go to the inauguration of the Suez Canal first and then proceed up the Nile . . . describe whatever is interesting for tourists. . . . Then you might as well go to Jerusalem. . . . Then visit Constantinople, and find out about that trouble between the Khedive and the Sultan. Then—let me see—you might as well visit the Crimea and those old battle grounds. Then go across the Caucasus to the Caspian Sea. . . . From there you may get through Persia to India; you could write an interesting letter from Persepolis.

"Bagdad will be close on your way to India; suppose you go there. . . . Then, when you have come to India, you can go after Livingstone. . . . Get what news of his discoveries you can; and, if you find he is dead, bring all possible proofs of his being dead. That is all. Good-night and God be with you."

Though Stanley had never been to Central Africa, Bennett could not possibly have chosen a better man for the job. Henry Stanley had already been in fifteen battles, three naval bombardments, and two shipwrecks. He had traveled tens of thousands of miles, usually alone, in freezing winter and scorching heat. He had endured a childhood that would have broken most men but had left him tough and absolutely fearless. Stanley had already accomplished so much that he was quite sure he could carry out Bennett's unusual task successfully, and if he did not, he was perfectly ready to die in the attempt.

To this point Henry Stanley's life had been one of remarkable adventure—and yet the real adventure had just begun.

CHAPTER 5

Livingstone

Who was Dr. David Livingstone, the man who played so large a part in Stanley's life? Livingstone was a missionary who made only one convert. He was an explorer who completely misinterpreted his own discoveries. He was an opponent of the slave trade who often depended on slavers for his very life. He denounced modern industrial civilization but thought it would bring salvation to Africa. He promoted Western Christian values, yet he preferred the company of Africans and sometimes ran at the approach of a white man. He was called a saint by those who didn't know him, and an arrogant, obsessive crank by many of those who did know him. Livingstone was, wrote one of his biographers, "A Contradictory Hero."

But he was certainly a hero. Livingstone had come from a background nearly as hideous as Stanley's. His family had been desperately poor, and David had been put to work in the Scottish cotton mills at the age of ten. Like other mill children he worked twelve hours a day, six days a week, and was beaten if his attention to his work lapsed, even for a moment. Less than 10 percent of the children put to work in the mills ever learned to read and write. Yet Livingstone not only learned but also mastered Latin, botany, theology, and some mathematics. With money he had been able to save from his miserable wages and with a bit of help from his family, he was able to enter Anderson's College in Glasgow. Livingstone was virtually the only child, of the hundreds of thousands who were sent to work in the mills, who ever received an advanced education. By merely surviving, Livingstone had already proved himself to be a remarkable individual.

Livingstone was deeply religious, and it had been his intention to become a medical missionary in China. But just as he was about to embark for China, the Chinese Opium War broke out, and he went to South Africa instead. In 1845 Livingstone established the most remote mission on the African continent and began a series of explorations of the interior of Africa. Livingstone knew that he was not a particularly good missionary, but because of his toughness, determination, and genuinely sympathetic interest in peoples of other cultures he made an excellent explorer. He hoped that his explorations would open the way for other missionaries. For the next twenty years he explored large portions of the African interior, and his reports gained him considerable fame in Europe.

In 1864 Livingstone returned to England and announced his intention to retire. The Royal Geographical Society persuaded him to return to Africa once more to see if he could clear up some geographical questions about Central Africa, particularly about the ultimate source of the Nile. At the time Livingstone was fifty-two, and though he had a good constitution, his years in Africa had begun to tell, and he was far from a well man. Yet he immediately agreed to go. Livingstone had come to look upon exploration as his mission; besides, he didn't much like England.

In December 1866, there was a report that Livingstone had died in Central Africa. The report was widely believed, and his obituary was published in leading newspapers throughout the world. Then letters from Livingstone dated February 1867 and July 1868 were brought out of the interior. After that there was silence, and rumors of Livingstone's death again began to circulate.

It would be a mistake to say that the world held its breath awaiting further news of Livingstone. In fact, in October 1869, when Bennett gave Stanley his commission to find Livingstone, the Scottish missionary was pretty much a forgotten figure. It was Bennett's journalistic genius that made him realize that a personal, firsthand interview with this man would be a great coup for the *Herald* and an event of enormous interest to the world. Livingstone was to be far more famous after Stanley found him than he was before.

Bennett's decision to send Stanley on other assignments before embarking on his expedition to the interior of Africa was also not just a caprice. The last authentic news of Livingstone was in July 1868. It was always possible that within a few months the missionary would appear on the coast, and the *Herald* expedition would be a washout, even an embarrassment. But if Livingstone were to remain "lost" until, say, 1871, then the chances were good that he would not suddenly appear, and people would want to know what had happened to him. It was a gamble, but one that paid off brilliantly for Bennett, for Livingstone, and most of all for Stanley.

Stanley followed all of Bennett's instructions. From Egypt he described the mummy vendors of Thebes who chased tourists down the street crying, "Buy a nice foot, sir!" In Jerusalem he was shocked by the commercialization of the Holy Places. Stanley visited Constantinople and looked up Edward Joy Morris, the American minister who had loaned Stanley £150 after his ill-fated Turkish expedition. Stanley tried to make good on his worthless check, but Morris insisted he had already been paid back. Morris was impressed with the change that had taken place in Stanley: "The uncouth young man whom I first knew had grown into a perfect man of the world, possessing the appearance, the manners and the attributes of a perfect gentleman. . . ." Morris, who became a great admirer of Stanley's, exaggerated, but there is no doubt that at the age of twenty-six the former workhouse boy had become rather worldly. Still, when he traveled through Russia, the loose morality displayed at a carnival in Odessa upset him terribly. In sexual matters Stanley could never be worldly.

Stanley traveled to Persia and India, and finally on January 6, 1871, some fifteen months after his meeting with Bennett, Stanley arrived on the island of Zanzibar ready to start his search for Livingstone. He had not been in touch with Bennett for some time and had a mere eighty dollars in his pocket. He had never organized an expedition before, but he borrowed large sums of money and set about doing so.

The Arab-controlled island of Zanzibar had always been the chief port for exports from the interior of Africa—primarily slaves and ivory—and the jumping-off place for expeditions. Stanley tried to keep the object of his expedition secret, but he aroused the suspicions of Sir John Kirk, the British consul. Stanley was spending thousands of dollars to equip an expedition, allegedly to explore a small and obscure African river. America and Britain were not on the friendliest of terms at that time, and the Englishman wondered what Stanley was up to. If Sir John had known the real object of the Stanley expedition, he probably would have been more helpful, for he was a friend of Livingstone's. In fact, Sir John Kirk didn't really think Livingstone was "lost" at all. When, without disclosing his real intentions, Stanley tried to ask Sir John about the missionary explorer, he was told that Livingstone hated publicity and probably didn't want to be bothered. Sir John said Livingstone would probably avoid any contact with another white man. Stanley wrongly interpreted this as a sign of Sir John's indifference to his old friend.

Stanley was lucky that the U.S. consul in Zanzibar was the extremely competent Captain Francis R. Webb, to whom Stanley confided the true purpose of his mission. Webb not only helped Stanley organize the expedition but helped him borrow the money for it, fully confident that Bennett would make good all debts, which he did. Ultimately the expedition cost over $20,000, an enormous sum in 1871.

Organizing an expedition into the interior of Africa was a complex undertaking. Take, for example, the matter of beads, cloth, and wire. These items were not mere trinkets to be used as gifts for the "primitive" natives. They served as currency for the various tribes, and different tribes were quite specific about the type of currency they used. Just as it would be impossible to buy a hamburger in the United States with a handful of French francs, it would have been impossible to buy food in Unyamwezi with black beads. There, red beads were the currency; black beads were useful in Ugogo.

It was necessary to have sufficient supplies, but not too much, for everything had to be carried to the interior. There were no roads and no carts. There were few pack animals, and they usually succumbed quickly to the tsetse fly. Stanley collected about six tons of supplies for his expedition. This load was to be carried primarily by 157 *pagazis*, or bearers. In addition there were 23 armed *askaris*, or guards, and 5 additional men with miscellaneous duties. Even before he arrived in Zanzibar, Stanley was accompanied by an Arab boy named Selim, whom he had met in Palestine and who was to serve as interpreter, and a Scots seaman named William Farquhar. In Zanzibar, Stanley hired an English sailor, John Shaw.

The expedition finally set off from the town of Bagamoyo on the eastern coast of Africa on March 21, 1871. Since Stanley had no idea where Livingstone actually was at that moment, indeed whether Livingstone was even alive, he had no set destination. His idea was simply to head toward that area in which Livingstone was last known to have been, and hope to pick up further news along the way. The place where Livingstone had last been heard from was Ujiji, some 750 miles inland.

Though there was dense jungle on the coast, most of the route ran through open plateau known as savanna. Stanley's expedition was not marching off into a trackless and unknown wilderness. Stanley was following a caravan route that had been used for centuries by Arab traders and slavers and by other European explorers. Though Stanley had never led an expedition before, he was an experienced traveler, and he possessed a talent for leadership. At first, he quite enjoyed himself. He had a single, clear purpose—to find Livingstone, and he liked being away from all the other problems of the world. "All I had to do was to free my mind from all else, and relieve it of every earthly desire but finding of the man whom I was sent to seek." Stanley was utterly convinced that he would succeed. In his diary he wrote, "No living man, or living men, shall stop me, only death can prevent me. But death—not even this; I shall not die, I will not die, I cannot die!"

To complete the task successfully, Stanley needed all his willpower. Though he traveled a known route and the tribes along the way were not hostile, they were not inclined to be particularly cooperative either. Each chief demanded payment for passage through his territory, and this was the subject of endless negotiations. Stanley displayed great patience and skill. His memories of observing negotiations with the Indians of America served him well.

There was a major war going on between the Arabs and a chief named Mirambo. The route to Ujiji was partially blocked, and Stanley was forced to make a wide detour and fight a few battles. The fear of being caught in the middle of the war frightened men of Stanley's into trying to desert. However, no new pagazis could be found who were willing to enter the war zone.

Temperatures along the way were often over 120 degrees, and during the rainy season much of the march was carried out in knee-deep mud and slime. Crossing swollen rivers was exhausting and dangerous.

Insects were more than an annoyance, they spread diseases like malaria. Stanley was laid low with repeated attacks of fever, some so severe that he was unconscious or delirious for days. There were other diseases—

dysentery, smallpox, and the dreaded elephantiasis. Farquhar was a victim of that disease, and his legs swelled up to several times their normal size.

Since no expedition could possibly carry enough food, they had to find food along the way, and often there was none. "Starving HMS," Stanley carved on the trunk of a tree after marching several days with almost no food.

All these hardships thoroughly demoralized the expedition. There were desertions and constant threats of mutiny. By September Stanley was opposed by practically everyone in the expedition except Selim, and he had to force the men back to work at gunpoint. Farquhar and Shaw were great disappointments to Stanley—they were brutal, sullen, and worst of all, they wanted to give up. Stanley would not hear of it, so at one point Shaw fired his rifle into the tent where Stanley was sleeping. Stanley chose to ignore the incident. Farquhar became so ill that he had to be left behind at a village, along with enough supplies to get him back to the coast as soon as he was well enough. A few days later he said he was well enough to go, got up, and then fell down dead. When Stanley heard of the death he said, "There is one of us gone, Shaw my boy! Who will be next?"

By this time Shaw, who was suffering from syphilis among other diseases, was practically insane. Stanley alternately babied him and became infuriated by him. Shaw kept begging to be left behind, but Stanley urged him on. When Shaw fell off his donkey and said he was too weak to get on the donkey again, Stanley left him lying there in the hot sun for over an hour. Yet that evening Shaw and Stanley sat together and sang "Home Sweet Home" and other songs—Stanley practically cried. Stanley now realized that Shaw simply could not continue, so on September 13 he left him in a village with supplies enough to last several months. Perhaps Shaw would be able to recover his strength and be picked up on the way back. However, Shaw died a few days after Stanley left.

Despite all these hardships, Stanley made excellent time. He covered the route twice as fast as earlier travelers, and along the way he had picked up vague rumors of Livingstone. Early in November, Stanley received his first definite word of Livingstone. A caravan coming from Ujiji reported that a white man had just arrived there.

"Is he young or old?" Stanley asked.

"He is old. He has white hair on his face, and is sick."

"Where has he come from?"

"From a very far country away beyond Uguhha, called Manyuema."

"Was he ever at Ujiji before?"

"Yes, he went away a long time ago."

Stanley could not believe his good fortune. It was Livingstone without a doubt, and he had returned to the very spot toward which Stanley had been heading. He was exhilarated—but frightened. Would Livingstone run away as Sir John Kirk had suggested? Would he be cold and uncooperative? Stanley had had many rebuffs in his life. Perhaps it wasn't Livingstone after all. He could not wait; Stanley promised his men extra pay if they would march even more quickly.

On November 10, 1871, Henry Morton Stanley, dressed in his best clothes and preceded by his gigantic guide Asmani, who carried the American flag on the end of a long boar spear, strode into Ujiji. Two of Livingstone's servants came out to greet the newcomers. They asked Stanley's name and rushed to tell the doctor. The name Henry Morton Stanley was meaningless to him. Livingstone was seated with a group of Arabs.

Selim shouted, "I see the doctor, sir. Oh what an old man! He has got a white beard."

Stanley was fairly bursting with excitement: "What would I not have given for a bit of some friendly wilderness, where unseen I might vent my joy in some mad freak, such as idiotically biting my hand, turning a somersault, or slashing at trees, in order to allay those exciting feelings that were well-nigh uncontrollable."

Stanley wanted to run and embrace the old man, but he recalled Livingstone was an Englishman. "I did not know how he would receive me." Stanley tried to be dignified, to act as a proper Englishman might act. He walked deliberately forward, took off his hat, and said:

"Dr. Livingstone, I presume?"

The old man lifted his cap slightly and said, "Yes."

The two shook hands, and Stanley said, "I thank God, Doctor, I have been permitted to see you."

Livingstone answered, "I feel thankful that I am here to welcome you."

That scene is the most famous in the history of African exploration. Even today, if a person knows nothing else of Stanley or Livingstone, he or she is likely to have heard the line "Dr. Livingstone, I presume." The line became so famous that Stanley wished he had never uttered it. It was incorporated into songs and music hall routines. No matter where Stanley went later in life, someone was sure to come up to him, stick out a hand, and say, "Mr. Stanley, I presume." In 1890 when Stanley was being given an honorary degree by Oxford University—a very solemn occasion—an undergraduate suddenly yelled out, "Dr. Stanley, I presume." Everyone laughed, everyone except Stanley, who could never fathom why others found the remark funny. Why had he said it? Stanley was trying to act and sound like a proper Englishman—which he was not. "I couldn't think what else to say," he once admitted.

But at the moment of the meeting the remark did not loom so large. Stanley had come at an ideal time. Livingstone had been ill, and he was nearly out of supplies and almost desperate. At another time he might have run from a reporter, but at that moment the arrival of this unknown American was a godsend to him, and he was extremely grateful.

At the end of that day Stanley wrote in his diary: "Indescribably happy."

There were a few uncomfortable moments, such as when Stanley asked Livingstone if he had ever heard of the New York *Herald*.

"Oh, who hasn't heard of that despicable newspaper?" replied Livingstone. When he was told that Bennett of the *Herald* had sent Stanley to find Livingstone, the doctor changed. "Well, indeed! I am very much obliged to him; and it makes me feel proud to think that you Americans think so much of me. . . ."

In fact, Livingstone genuinely liked the courageous young reporter, and Stanley was simply awed by Livingstone, whom he immediately regarded as a living saint. The missionary was second only to his adoptive father in Stanley's eyes.

After a few months Stanley began to suspect that Livingstone wasn't quite the saint he had believed him to be; "but I have been driving [such thoughts] steadily from my mind. . . ." What bothered Stanley was Livingstone's bitterness and inability to forget or forgive old quarrels. Yet during his lifetime Stanley never published a word of complaint about Livingstone; his doubts were expressed only to his private diary.

Stanley's food and medicine helped restore Livingstone's health; the news that the outside world had not forgotten him restored his spirits. The two men did some exploring together around the northern end of Lake Tanganyika. Stanley was still suffering from recurrent fevers, and sometimes it seemed as if he, not Livingstone, was the really sick man. Stanley wrote in his diary:

"Am carried again as I cannot even ride by donkey. I am in such a state tonight that I can neither lie down or sit quietly in one position long. Livingstone is calmly asleep—I am nervous and my head is very strange. I have the most fearful dreams every night and am afraid to shut my eyes lest I shall see the horrid things that haunt me. I will go walk, walk, walk in the forest to get rid of them." Massive doses of quinine often put Stanley in this frightful state.

Livingstone was extremely tough. During one march he was stung horribly by a swarm of bees. His donkey was killed by the bees. Despite the pain, Livingstone insisted on marching on, and when Stanley sent back two men with a hammock to carry him, Livingstone was furious. The old missionary could be alarming when angry; Stanley was careful to steer clear of him until later that evening.

Despite his toughness Livingstone was far from a well man. Stanley tried to persuade him to return with him, but Livingstone would not hear of it. He had the notion that a river called the Lualaba was the source of the Nile, and he said that he was going to stay in Africa until he proved it. It is also probable that Livingstone, who had spent so much of his life in Africa, had decided to die there.

Livingstone gave Stanley a tin box of letters, journals, and other papers, which were to be taken to the outside world. Among the letters were two for Bennett, expressing his gratitude for sending Stanley. Stanley declared that when he reached the coast he would personally see that additional supplies were sent to Livingstone, so that he could continue his quest for the source of the Nile.

It was decided that Stanley would leave on March 14, 1872, the end of the rainy season. Those who had come out with Stanley were overjoyed at the prospect of returning home. They gave a farewell dance at which Stanley, waving a spear, jumped about like a madman to the sound of drums. Yet Stanley had mixed emotions about leaving Livingstone. When the moment of final parting actually came, Stanley broke down and cried.

The trip back to the coast was far easier than the trip inland had been. Most of the supplies had already been used or turned over to Livingstone, so there was less to carry. The pagazis who were now heading homeward had no reason to desert and every reason to hurry. The war between the Arabs and Mirambo had ebbed, and the route was clear. Still, travel across Africa was never easy. Though the rainy season was supposed to have ended, it rained almost constantly, resulting in swollen rivers, newly made swamps, and hordes of black mosquitoes that made sleeping almost impossible.

For Stanley there was one frightening moment. On April 13 the expedition was crossing a narrow but deep river. A tree had been cut down to span the river, and most of the men were slowly making their way across this makeshift bridge. One of the younger pagazis, impatient with the slow progress, plunged into the river and fell into a hole up to his neck. This particular man was carrying the tin box containing all of Livingstone's papers. Stanley watched in horror. The whole success of his mission depended on his bringing those papers back. He whipped out his pistol and shouted to the man in the river, "Look out! Drop that box and I'll shoot you." Then he held his breath as the terrified man slowly and carefully made his way to safety with the box intact. Stanley quickly entrusted the prize to an older and more cautious guardian.

On the evening of May 6 the Stanley expedition reached the town of Bagamoyo from which it had departed fourteen months before. Stanley had the now-tattered American flag hoisted on a spear, and the men fired off the last of the ammunition to announce their arrival.

In total, the expedition had been away 411 days and had traveled 2,250 miles. Eighteen Africans and two Britons had died during the ordeal. Stanley himself had lost seventy-six pounds because of an acute attack of dysentery and twenty-three bouts with severe fever. His round face had become gaunt, and his thick black hair was now streaked with gray. He had aged ten years.

Yet he had done what he set out to do—he had found Livingstone. Now he hoped to reap the rewards of his remarkable success.

Pictures from the Works of Henry Stanley

At age fifteen John Rowlands was a chubby boy.

The St. Asaph Union Workhouse, the grim institution where Rowlands spent most of his youth.

Taken shortly after the Livingstone expedition, this picture shows Stanley in his explorer's garb.

James Gordon Bennett, Jr., publisher of the New York *Herald*.

The harbor at the island of Zanzibar, as Stanley saw it in 1871 on his way to find Livingstone.

anley's camp at Bagamoyo on the east coast of Africa, opposite Zanzibar.

John Shaw and William Farquhar, Stanley's two European companions on the Livingstone expedition.

Stanley's expedition crosses the Makata swamp in 1871.

"Dr. Livingstone, I presume?" The most famous scene in all African exploration.

Livingstone at work on his journal. Though Stanley described Livingstone as an old man with white hair, this picture based on Stanley's own drawing shows him looking more youthful.

Stanley and Livingstone exploring Lake Tanganyika, shortly before the two parted.

Stanley and his men in Zanzibar in 1877, after they had explored the Congo River.

The notorious slave trader Tippu Tib, as he looked at the time of the Emin Pasha expedition.

Emin Pasha. With his fez, it was said he looked like a German doctor at a Shriner's convention.

Dorothy Tennant Stanley, the explorer's wife and protector in his later years.

Stanley's massive headstone in the village churchyard in Pirbright.

CHAPTER 6

The Celebrity

Henry Morton Stanley was essentially a simple man. In finding Livingstone he had accomplished something truly extraordinary. He expected that the world would recognize his accomplishment and make him rich, famous, and happy. That seemed to be simple justice. He did become rich and famous, but happiness eluded him, for the world was not nearly as simple as Stanley believed it to be.

While Stanley was in Africa and out of touch, many things had changed in the outside world; one of the changes was the public's attitude toward Livingstone. After Livingstone's letter of late 1869, the British public assumed that the missionary-explorer was safe. But by 1871 he had not been heard of for a long time, and fears for his life were again widely expressed. News of the war between Arabs and Mirambo deepened these fears, since the war was taking place in the region where Livingstone was thought to be exploring.

Then there was the *Herald* expedition. Though Stanley tried to keep the purpose of his foray into Central Africa secret, it soon became known. What really bothered the people of Britain about this expedition was that it was sponsored by the New York *Herald*, a sensationalistic newspaper that, moreover, was often very hostile to Britain.

If a vulgar upstart American like James Gordon Bennett could equip an expedition to find a British hero, could the Royal Geographical Society do any less? Especially since the Royal Geographical Society had sent Livingstone back to Africa in the first place. The society decided that it could not, and on New Year's Day 1872 it announced the formation of the Livingstone Search and Relief Expedition. Of course, by that time Stanley and Livingstone were paddling around Lake Tanganyika together and having a wonderful time.

News of the meeting of Stanley and Livingstone began to filter out of Central Africa early in 1872. At first the news was simply not believed. Bennett's paper had printed false stories in the past, and this was assumed to be just another one of them. Plans for the Livingstone Search and Relief Expedition went forward, though in a rather muddled way.

As information about Stanley and Livingstone grew firmer, a number of wild rumors circulated. One was that Stanley had been trapped by Mirambo and was rescued by Livingstone. Another was that Stanley had not actually met Livingstone but had purchased the box of letters and diaries, which had been stolen from Livingstone.

When Stanley walked into Bagamoyo on May 6, 1872, the first man to greet him was young William Henn, second in command of the Royal Geographical

Society expedition. Llewellyn Dawson, leader of the expedition, upon learning that Stanley had actually located Livingstone, was so infuriated that he resigned and was too angry to go out and greet Stanley.

Some of the letters that Livingstone had given to Stanley contained bombshells. Livingstone was not a man to forget or forgive any offense, real or imagined. His letter to his old friend Sir John Kirk in Zanzibar was full of bitter complaints. He practically accused Sir John of stealing money meant for his supplies. Sir John Kirk, who had genuinely wished Stanley well, was furious. He thought that Stanley had poisoned Livingstone's mind, and he went so far as to call Livingstone a "damned old scoundrel." That shocked other members of the expedition.

Oswell Livingstone, one of the doctor's sons, was part of the relief expedition. Stanley had brought some letters for him as well. When Oswell read them he felt so "disgusted and ashamed" that he resigned. Stanley lectured him on filial piety—despite this, Stanley and young Livingstone got on quite well.

There were many matters to clear up in Africa, including organizing another relief expedition for Livingstone, since the Royal Geographical Society expedition had dissolved in anger and controversy. It wasn't until July 24 that Stanley again returned to Europe. He landed at Marseilles and the next day was in Paris, where he found he was indeed a celebrity.

Everyone wanted to know who this Henry Stanley was. There were already several theories circulating. One theory held he was an imposter and a fraud. Another indicated he was Lord Stanley, son of the Earl of Derby. Some French papers even carried a story reprinted from a Welsh newspaper, which stated that

Henry Stanley was really a Welshman named John Rowlands from Denbigh and that his mother ran a pub. Stanley denied this last story (though it was quite true) and insisted that he was pure American. For years Stanley attempted to publicly deny, or at least obscure, his own humble origins.

He was besieged by reporters, and he spoke freely of his adventures in Africa. Bennett was becoming angry. The *Herald* had paid for the expedition, and the *Herald* should have exclusive rights to the fruits of the expedition. Stanley should not be giving other papers for free what the *Herald* had spent so much to obtain. He sent Stanley a telegram of two words: STOP TALKING.

Stanley spent six days in Paris being wined and dined by the large American colony. He expected that when he went to England his reception would be even warmer—but he was quite wrong. When he reached Dover there was not a single British official there to meet him. The welcoming committee consisted of two poor relations from Denbigh, who didn't even recognize him.

In England there was still a strong suspicion that the whole Stanley and Livingstone business was just another New York *Herald* fraud. Mark Twain, who happened to be in London at the time, confused everybody by joking that *he* had found Livingstone but didn't mind that his old friend Stanley was taking credit for it.

Stanley had to appeal to Livingstone's family to certify the genuineness of the letters that he brought from the doctor. He also asked Lord Granville, head of the Foreign Office, to confirm some official dispatches. Lord Granville wrote back immediately, saying that he had no idea that anyone had doubts about the dispatches, and of course they were genuine. Stanley had that letter published in the London *Times*, in order to silence his critics.

Lord Granville's letter forced the Royal Geographical Society to do something that it had been avoiding— recognize Stanley's accomplishment. The society was extremely embarrassed by the collapse of its own expedition. Society president Sir Henry Rawlinson had made some careless public remarks in which he had doubted Stanley's stories. Sir Henry was wrong and he didn't want to admit it. But he sent Stanley an official if belated letter of congratulations and invited him to address a meeting of the prestigious British association at Brighton. The night of the meeting the hall was packed with a very distinguished audience, including exiled Emperor Napoleon III of France.

Rawlinson opened the proceedings and said that he hoped Stanley would clear up certain mysteries about himself. When a very nervous Henry Stanley stepped up to the rostrum to speak, he was greeted with a burst of applause. Stanley was no speaker. He had a weak voice and a tendency to ramble or become overexcited. The geographers in the audience had expected a fact-filled dissertation on Central Africa. Instead, Stanley began: "I consider myself in the light of a Troubador, to relate to you the tale of an old man who is tramping onward to discover the source of the Nile."

Some of the members of the audience smiled, but Stanley continued on in the same flowery vein, telling of his travels and his experiences with Livingstone. Then he turned on Rawlinson and attacked him for asking personal questions about his origins.

After the speech, a number of the geographers in the audience raised objections to Livingstone's theories about the source of the Nile. Stanley attacked these geographers. How could anyone living in comfort in London dare question the word of a man who had spent thirty-five years in Africa? Stanley took any criticism of Living-stone as a personal insult. The bulk of the audience, who were not professional geographers, enjoyed themselves hugely. They liked to see a good fight in which some stuffy old professors had their arrogance punctured. Stanley carried the day but didn't realize it. He was far too sensitive to be able to bear the disapproval of the professionals, and he felt humiliated.

The next night was even worse because he attended a small but elegant banquet given by a medical society. Stanley was asked to say a few words, but he got carried away. There he stood, squeezed into evening dress, which never fit him properly; his face glowed red, his hair was falling over his eyes, and his arms were waving as he piped out in his American accent exaggerated praise of Livingstone and of his own accomplishments. The very stiff and proper British doctors were amazed and embarrassed at this performance. Then someone laughed loudly. Stanley froze. He turned on his audience with fury. He said he was being treated badly because he was an American. Livingstone had never cared about his na-tionality. Stanley shouted that he had been insulted enough, and he stalked out of the room.

Later he wrote: "All the actions of my life, and I may say all my thoughts, since 1872, have been strongly col-oured by the storm of abuse and the wholly unjustifiable reports circulated about me then."

Stanley was a prickly character—a porcupine, one of his friends called him, and he didn't disagree. In fact, he was a real hero to the British public, and a number of influential people felt that he really had been treated badly and tried to make up for it. The foreign secretary, Lord Granville, sent him, on Queen Victoria's behalf, a beautiful gold and jeweled snuffbox with the royal cipher

VR on it. Stanley loved counting the diamonds on the box. There were more than five dozen. He was also presented to the queen. It was a triumphant moment for Stanley; the queen asked him questions about his journey, and they spoke for about ten minutes. Stanley was deeply moved. He would have been less moved if he had known the queen's private opinion, for she really was a snob: "I have this evng. seen Mr. Stanley, who discovered Livingstone, a determined, ugly little Man—with a strong American twang."

Stanley would have been particularly insulted by being called little. He had always been sensitive about his height and was delighted to discover that the queen was even shorter than he was. He could look her in the eye, and that put him at ease. But he never knew; the snuffbox was one of his treasures, and the meeting with Queen Victoria one of his fondest memories.

Accompanying Stanley at most of his public appearances and creating almost as much interest as the explorer himself was a young African boy named Kalulu. Kalulu was a slave who had been given to Stanley in Africa. Stanley had renamed him Kalulu, the Swahili term for the young of the blue-buck antelope, in a ceremony reminiscent of the one in which his own name had been changed. He also informally adopted Kalulu, as he had once been informally adopted.

In Europe and later in America, Kalulu was regarded as something of a curiosity, like the spears and shields that Stanley had also brought back from Africa. But Stanley himself had a genuine fatherly affection for the boy.

Stanley was preparing to return to America; his articles about his adventures had already boosted the circulation of the New York *Herald* and made his employer,

James Gordon Bennett, Jr., richer than ever. But Stanley's fame was beginning to irritate Bennett. As a rule, the names of *Herald* correspondents were never even mentioned in the paper. All the credit was to go to the *Herald*—and to Bennett. In this case Stanley's name could hardly be left out. When Stanley was presented to the queen, it really annoyed him. Bennett hated the British monarchy, anyway. Then he heard that Stanley was going to receive fifty thousand dollars for a lecture tour. That was more than the whole Livingstone expedition cost! Bennett believed that the money rightly belonged to the *Herald*, which had given him the chance to go to Africa in the first place. Stanley had been a lowly reporter before the expedition, and Bennett had paid all the bills.

By the time Stanley was scheduled to arrive in New York, Bennett was in a rage, but there was so much excitement about the new hero he had to curb his anger. To fire or humiliate Stanley at that moment would have been stupid.

Besides, Bennett was busy publicly defending Stanley from attacks by rival newspapers. The New York *Sun* hired Stanley's old traveling companion Louis Noe to denounce him as a brute, swindler, a forger, and a Welshman. Stanley denied it all, and the *Herald* said that Stanley was born in Missouri, not Wales.

When Stanley finally arrived on November 20, Bennett treated him like a prince. But the publisher could not tolerate anyone else in his organization having any power or prestige, so he waited to cut Stanley down to size. He got his chance at Stanley's lectures. The first New York lecture was scheduled for December 3. It was sold out long in advance, and on the night of the lecture scalpers were getting five times the original cost on tickets.

At Brighton, Stanley felt he had made a fool of him-self by getting carried away. He was determined not to have the same thing happen again, so he carefully wrote out a speech filled with facts and figures. Stanley speak-ing extemporaneously was bad, but Stanley reading was far, far worse. The speech, which was two hours long, was incredibly boring. There was not a single adventur-ous, amusing, or personal story in it. Stanley gripped the rostrum, stared fixedly down at his notes, and read on and on in his thin weak voice. Only those sitting in the front ten rows could hear him, and when he looked up for the first time, to take a sip of water, after ninety minutes, Stanley saw that all but those sitting in the first ten rows had left, and those that remained were strug-gling to stay awake.

The lecture was a disaster, and this disaster was com-pounded by the presence of *Herald* reporter George O. Seilhamer, one of Bennett's toadies. Seilhamer had never been told what to do, but he knew his boss's mind well enough. His review of Stanley's lecture was cutting. The audience, he said "was a little too well bred to be very eagerly enthusiastic." Seilhamer was again in the audi-ence the next evening, when Stanley delivered an even drier and more boring talk. Once again Stanley was roasted in the pages of the *Herald*, this time even more fiercely: "Mr. Stanley's elocution is bad. . . ."

Stanley didn't know what was happening to him. He couldn't understand how Bennett would allow this. Ben-nett did call Seilhamer in and reprimand him lightly, but had he really been angry, he would have fired the re-porter on the spot. "I could see that he was really gratified," said Seilhamer.

Stanley's third lecture was so poorly attended that he was forced to cancel his fourth. The great lecture tour died before it really got started. Stanley felt sick and humiliated. He tried to complain to Bennett, but the publisher had already left for Paris on his private yacht. It was said that as he walked up the gangplank he winked at George O. Seilhamer.

Though Stanley failed as a lecturer, his book *How I Found Livingstone* was a success. Somehow he had managed to write the massive seven-hundred-page volume in the hectic months after his return from Africa. He even illustrated it with copies of his own excellent drawings. The book was published before he left England and was an instant best-seller there and in America. There were criticisms of the book's rather stilted style. "It is, without exception, the very worst book on the very best subject, I ever saw in all my life," wrote Florence Nightingale. "Still I can't help devouring it to the end." Oddly, Stanley was not at all sensitive about his writing and told his publishers that the critics had treated him kindly and were not half as severe as he would have been. As a journalist, Stanley was a lively writer. When he sat down to write a book, he tried to sound literary but succeeded only in sounding pompous.

The Livingstone expedition had made Stanley famous, but there were a lot of celebrities in New York, and by early 1873 Henry Stanley had slipped back once more into the role of anonymous journalist for the New York *Herald*.

In late April Stanley was in England when he received another summons from Bennett in Paris. He arrived at Bennett's hotel on May 2 and was given a new assignment: he was to go back to Spain to cover another of the series of revolts that seemed to be endlessly convulsing that country. Bennett was in a bad temper and refused to give Stanley a raise. Stanley was angry but confided his feelings only to his diary. He said nothing to Bennett.

Stanley was in Spain when a more interesting assignment came up. The British were launching a military expedition in the part of West Africa now called Ghana, this time against the Ashantis, who had been harassing tribes under British protection. This was part of a conflict between the British and the Ashantis that had been going on for half a century. Stanley rushed off to Africa to cover the war for the *Herald*.

He arrived before the war began. The British were not yet ready to march, and Stanley had nothing to do. Inactivity always put him in a terrible mood, and his early dispatches were filled with complaints about everything and everybody. When the war finally began, it was very one-sided. The Ashantis were extremely brave, but they were no match for a modern army. The British entered village after village with ease. It was not, in Stanley's view, a very exciting war though he did his best to try to make it sound exciting in his articles. By the end of February 1874 the war was over and Stanley headed back to Europe and an uncertain future. He was on a ship when he learned of Livingstone's death.

Livingstone had died on May 1, 1873, near Lake Bangweolo. He was still searching for the source of the Nile. Some of his followers had dried the explorer's body and carried it back to the coast. The journey had taken months. The outside world did not hear of Livingstone's fate until early 1874.

The news of the missionary-explorer's death created a sensation. Since his dramatic meeting with Stanley, Livingstone had become more famous than ever. Stanley's writings, which treated the doctor as a living saint, had done more than anything else to build the Livingstone legend and make him a national hero. When his body arrived at Southampton on April 15, 1874, there was a crowd of fifty thousand on hand. His funeral three days later was one of the grandest that had ever been seen in England. Livingstone was laid to rest in Westminster Abbey, the prime burial place of English heroes. Henry Stanley was one of the pallbearers.

Stanley was deeply moved: "Dear Livingstone! Another sacrifice to Africa! His mission, however, must not be allowed to cease; others must go forward and fill the gap."

Stanley decided that he was going to fill that gap; he was going to finish Livingstone's work of exploration. A few days later Stanley outlined his plans to Edward Levy-Lawson, owner of the British newspaper the *Daily Telegraph*. He wanted to lead an expedition to Central Africa that would, among other things, finally settle the question of the source of the Nile and the mystery of the Lualaba River, which Livingstone had always believed was the Nile. Stanley proposed that the *Telegraph* sponsor the expedition.

Lawson was intrigued, but the *Telegraph* alone could not bear the expense of such an undertaking. "Well, well! I will cable over to Bennett of the New York *Herald* and ask if he is willing to join in this expedition of yours," said Lawson.

Bennett in New York read the cable and sent back a characteristically to-the-point reply: "YES. BENNETT."

CHAPTER 7

The Nyanza

Henry Stanley had three basic objectives in mind as he set out for his second African expedition. They all concerned the source of the Nile. It had been assumed that the Nile flowed out of a large lake in Central Africa. But which lake? There were two major possibilities.

The explorer Richard Burton held that the Nile flowed out of Lake Tanganyika. Burton's fellow explorer, and later his bitter enemy, John Hanning Speke, insisted that the Nile's source was another lake called Victoria Nyanza (Nyanza means lake). Burton and Speke had done their exploring in the late 1850s. Since the early 1860s most geographers had agreed with Speke, but still the controversy lingered. Burton insisted that Victoria Nyanza was not really a large lake at all but a mass of small lakes and swamps. The controversy kept boiling because no one had ever actually sailed around either lake. Stanley proposed to settle the problem once and for all by sailing around both lakes.

An even more intriguing problem was the Lualaba River. It was a very large river that flowed northward through the heart of Africa. Since the land was unmapped, no one knew where this great river began or ended. Livingstone had always believed it continued to flow north and was in fact the Nile itself. He had died trying to prove that theory. Naturally that was what Stanley believed as well. The majority of the geographers who had so humiliated Stanley at Brighton in 1872 contended that the Lualaba took a sharp westward turn and emptied into the Atlantic Ocean, and that it was really the Congo River. A few believed that it was the smaller Niger River. Stanley intended to settle this matter by sailing the length of the Lualaba.

It was an enormous undertaking, far more ambitious and much riskier than the search for Livingstone, for now Stanley intended to venture into territory that was completely unknown to the outside world. Other explorers, including Livingstone himself, had been unable to penetrate this region.

Before leaving England, Stanley read through the hundreds of letters from people who wanted to accompany him. He chose only three, two young brothers Frank and Edward Pocock, who had been bargemen and knew a good deal about small boats, and Frederick Barker, whose only qualifications were that he wanted to go to Africa and Stanley liked him. In organizing supplies and in planning routes and most other phases of an expedition, Stanley was meticulous. In choosing those who were to accompany him he tended to be impulsive and sentimental. But then there was really no way of telling in advance who would bear up well under the hardships of an expedition of this type, because there was no way of telling what the hardships would be.

Stanley arrived in Zanzibar in August of 1874 and quickly began to make preparations. He was a seasoned African traveler now, and he prepared his enterprise with confidence. If this expedition was to be concerned primarily with three bodies of water, then, of course, he would need boats. Stanley commissioned the construction of three boats, the largest of which he designed himself. It was forty feet long and six feet wide. He christened it the *Lady Alice*. Since the *Lady Alice*, like all other equipment, had to be carried to the interior, the boat was broken up into five eight-foot sections, each of which could be carried by two men. There were, in addition, guns and ammunition, medicine, some food, photographic and scientific equipment, and the usual beads, wire, and cloth to pay tribes for supplies along the way. All of this had to be carefully packed in boxes and bundles weighing from forty to seventy pounds.

In choosing men for the trip Stanley gave first priority to all veterans of the Livingstone Search Expedition or men who had served with Livingstone himself. The most experienced man was Manwa Sera, who had also been on expeditions headed by Speke and other European explorers. This veteran was made head chief. Other chiefs were also men known to Stanley. Many of them were allowed to bring their families on the expedition.

Three hundred and fifty-six men were finally selected, and events were to prove that, by and large, Stanley had chosen wisely. But it did not seem so at first. On November 12, 1874, Stanley's Anglo-American Expedition landed at the coastal town of Bagamoyo and some of the men immediately set about robbing and threatening the townsfolk. The guilty parties were soon identified, but so much ill will had been generated that Stanley was unable to recruit additional pagazis, and he headed off into the interior shorthanded. It was not an encouraging start.

The Anglo-American expedition began on the same familiar caravan route that Stanley had used when he found Livingstone. By December, however, the column had turned northward and was heading into unexplored territory, and into trouble. Because there was a famine in the land, it was difficult and sometimes impossible to purchase enough food, even for ten times the usual price. The inevitable accompaniments of near starvation were disease, death, and desertion. In less than two months' time, twenty people had died and eighty-nine deserted. Among the dead was Edward Pocock.

It was a weary, sick and starved line that entered the region known as Ituru, under what Stanley described as "a presentiment of evil." Up to this point the tribes that the expedition encountered had been indifferent and unfriendly, but not actively hostile. Now matters were different. One of the sick men fell behind the main column. When he was missed, a party went back to look for him and found he had been "hacked to little pieces and scattered along the road."

A few nights later two members of Stanley's expedition left camp to forage for fuel: "One was speared to death, the other rushed into camp, a lance quivering in his arm, his body gashed with the flying weapons, his face streaming with blood from the blow of a whirling knobstick."

Stanley's men urged him to fight, but he held back, telling them: "Even for this, I will not fight. . . . Two lives are lost; but that is a small loss compared with the loss of a hundred or even fifty. You cannot fight a tribe like this without paying a heavy forfeit of life. I cannot afford to lose you. We have a thousand tribes to go through yet, and you talk of war now. Be patient, men, this will blow over."

Though many of Stanley's men were well armed, they were not an army, and they were not equipped or trained to fight their way into the heart of Africa. To a very great degree the success of the expedition depended on the friendliness or at least the indulgence of the people through whose land they passed. Even when starvation threatened, Stanley would not allow his men to pillage. News of such activity would travel fast, and tribes farther along the route would be roused to hostility. But finally a direct attack on the expedition camp stirred Stanley to take action. He had his camp strongly fortified and then formed his best fighters into five detachments with orders to attack. The fighting was bitter and by late afternoon "[o]ur losses amounted to twenty-two killed, and three wounded. My effective force was now numbered two hundred and eight."

During the fight nearby villages were plundered. "The camp was full of cattle, goats, fowls, and grain. I could stand a siege for months, if necessary." However, a siege was not what Stanley wanted. The next day he sent out a strong force that pursued the enemy and burned their villages. The fury of the attack had taken the fight out of the opposing people, the expedition was now safe, but January had been a disastrous month. "I had lost a fourth of my effective force, with nearly seven thousand miles of a journey before me!"

There were not enough healthy men left in camp to carry the remaining loads. The amount of baggage had to be reduced. "Personal baggage, luxuries, books, cloth, beads, wire, extra tents, were freely sacrificed." Stanley, however, never lost sight of the purpose of his expedition, and he clung to the *Lady Alice*, though he admitted to being sorely tempted to leave her behind, because carrying her required so many men.

Then the expedition's luck changed. They entered friendly territory. With the cattle and goats they had captured in their fight, they were able to enlist the services of over a hundred additional pagazis, and on February 27, they reached the shores of Victoria Nyanza.

The bulk of the expedition was to camp at the shore while Stanley and a picked crew sailed the *Lady Alice* around the lake. He had some trouble picking the crew, for though his men had already proved themselves to be extremely brave, they knew nothing of sailing, and the very idea of it terrified them. Stanley asked for volunteers; when no one stepped forward, he was forced to select eleven unwilling crewmen: "I will make sailors of you, never fear! Get ready, we must be off within an hour."

It was a gloomy and gray March 8 when Stanley set out in the *Lady Alice*. "My crew sighed dolorously, and rowed like men abound to certain death. . . ."

The first part of the journey was relatively uneventful. They found a guide who frightened the crew with tales of the size of the lake. The guide said it would take years to sail around the lake and that no one would survive the journey. "On its shores dwelt a people with long tails; there was a tribe which trained big dogs for purposes of war; there were people, also, who preferred to feed on human beings rather than goats." None of this reassured the inexperienced and nervous crew. Neither did several violent storms, which nearly sank the *Lady Alice*. But slowly the men grew more comfortable and confident with their life on the water.

Victoria Nyanza, while it is nowhere near the size indicated by Stanley's gloomy guide, is the largest freshwater lake in Africa and, next to Lake Superior, the second largest lake in the world. It covers almost twenty-seven thousand square miles and has about two thousand miles of shoreline. Stanley was determined to record every cove and island in the lake and every river connected to it.

Early in April, Stanley approached the kingdom of Uganda, the best organized and largest state in Central Africa at that time. The kingdom had been in touch with the outside world for many years, and its king, Mtesa, had been converted to Islam by the Arabs. On his expedition in 1862, Speke had visited King Mtesa. The *Lady Alice* was met by a flotilla of decorated war canoes. As he approached the shore, Stanley saw a crowd that numbered in the thousands awaiting his arrival. Many carried colorful flags, and some of the men were dressed in gorgeous robes of red, black, and white. The men in the canoes fired off their muskets, and they were answered by musket shots from the shore. Scores of drums were being furiously beaten, and the masses on the shore were roaring shouts of welcome. It was a most friendly, impressive, and noisy reception.

Later that evening Stanley was introduced to King Mtesa himself. "I was ushered into the Imperial Presence through a multitude of chiefs, ranked in kneeling or seated lines, drummers, guards, executioners, and pages.

"Mtesa is slender and tall, probably six feet one inch in height. He has very intelligent and agreeable features which remind me of some of the faces of the great stone images at Thebes and of the statues in the Museum at Cairo. . . . His face is of a wonderfully smooth surface."

Mtesa wanted to talk of two things, Europe and Heaven. The king of Uganda was extremely curious about the Christian religion, particularly angels. Stanley threw himself into the work of explaining Christianity with great enthusiasm. "I may have exaggerated somewhat!" Mtesa liked what he heard, and before Stanley's visit of twelve days had ended, Mtesa had decided to observe the Christian as well as the Muslim Sabbath.

While in Uganda, Stanley met another European, Colonel Linant de Bellefonds, who had been sent by General Charles George "Chinese" Gordon, governor general of the Sudan, to establish official communications between the Sudan and Uganda. Stanley gave de Bellefonds some letters, including one to the *Telegraph* appealing for missionaries to Uganda. On his way back to the Sudan, de Bellefonds was murdered, and when his body was recovered, Stanley's letters were found concealed in his boots. The letters finally got to the *Telegraph*, where they were published in November 1875. They created a sensation and generated a huge flow of contributions for missionary work in Uganda. Mtesa, who was an effective but brutal ruler, was really less interested in European missionaries than in European technology.

Even though he stayed at Mtesa's court longer than he had anticipated, Stanley did not forget his main task, and he set off to explore the rest of Victoria Nyanza.

About ten days after leaving what Stanley called "that genial court," he encountered a very different reception on the island of Bumbireh. The *Lady Alice* came to the island where Stanley was looking for a place to rest and buy food, for they had run out of supplies and already had not eaten for thirty-six hours. The population of the island stood on the shore shouting war cries and waving their spears. The situation did not look promising, but Stanley felt he had overcome hostility before. Besides, as one of his men pointed out, "If we leave here without food, where shall we obtain it?"

That was a potent argument. So the boat was rowed slowly into shore while the interpreter stood in the bow yelling words of peace and friendship. These seemed to have an effect. Spears were lowered, and the people of Bumbireh shouted back words of friendship. A large party waded into the water, smiling and gesturing for the *Lady Alice* to come to shore. Then suddenly they grabbed hold of the boat and pulled it to the beach, dragging it about twenty yards from the water.

"Then ensued a scene of rampant wildness and hideous ferocity of action beyond description." The tiny crew of the *Lady Alice* was surrounded by a forest of spears and bows. The armed men seemed to be arguing with one another over who was to strike the first blow. Stanley with a pistol in each hand jumped up, ready to kill or be killed. "But as I rose to my feet, the utter hopelessness of our situation was revealed to me."

Stanley then adopted a tactic that he had learned from Livingstone. He became utterly calm, impassive, and unresisting. His men did the same, though several were beaten. Stanley himself did not escape. "They mistook my hair for a wig, and attempted to pull it off. They gave it such a wrench until the scalp tingled."

The islanders then grabbed the *Lady Alice*'s oars— legs, they called them—and carried them off. Stanley and his men were now stranded and helpless in a crowd that seemed quite ready to kill them. Yet the warriors of Bumbireh had not entirely decided what they were going to do. They withdrew for lunch and a conference. About three in the afternoon the war drums began beating and a line of warriors, their faces smeared with black and white pigments, appeared. "The most dull-witted amongst us knew what it portended!" said Stanley.

"A tall young fellow came bounding down the hill

and pounced on our Kinganda drum. It was only a curio we had picked up; we let them have it. Before going away he said, 'If you are men, prepare to fight.' "

At least the suspense was ended—Stanley felt there was no longer the possibility that he would be able to talk his way out of this. He sent his interpreter, Safeni, forward to create a diversion. He had his men grab hold of the *Lady Alice*. He then loaded his guns, "my elephant-rifle, double-barrelled shot gun, Winchester repeater, and two or three Sniders belonging to the men."

On Stanley's signal the men began to push like mad. "The boat moved, the crew drove her sternward, her keel ploughing through the gravel and crunching through the stony beach." Stanley shouted to Safeni, who turned and ran toward the water before the astonished islanders were quite sure what had happened. The crew had pushed the boat so fast that it had glided far out into the lake, and Safeni was forced to jump into the water and swim for it. The islanders, who had recovered from their surprise, rushed to the shore, but Stanley scattered them with a few shots. The islanders then launched their canoes, and since the *Lady Alice* had no oars, it could not outrace them; however, explosive bullets from Stanley's powerful elephant rifle were able to sink two canoes, and the rest turned back. As a parting taunt the islanders cried out, "Go and die in the Nyanza!"

It was not an idle threat. Stanley and his men were drifting in an open boat without oars, in hostile country, and they had not eaten for forty-nine hours. They hoisted their sail, but the wind was dead calm. They then broke some boards from the bottom of the boat and used them as improvised oars. The boards were weak and inadequate, but better than nothing.

The *Lady Alice* was heading for another island, where

Stanley and his men hoped to find food and shelter, when a series of violent storms erupted, drove them off course, and nearly sank the boat. Finally, two days later they managed to reach an uninhabited island. The men were exhausted from their ordeal and collapsed on the shore, but not for long, because they were also starving. "We shot some ducks, and discovered some wild fruit. Delicious evening—how we enjoyed it!"

They made some new oars, and three days later the *Lady Alice* was back at camp, having completed a circuit of Victoria Nyanza. As Speke had believed, Victoria Nyanza was a single large lake. It had only one main outlet to the north where the water rushed out of the lake over a series of cataracts that Speke named Ripon Falls and into a northward-flowing channel. This channel almost certainly became the Nile. Thus Stanley's exploration had finally settled one of the major questions about the source of the Nile. But there was still much more to do.

Stanley and his crew had been gone fifty-six days. In that time disease had broken out in the camp. Frederick Barker had died of a fever, as had five of the Zanzibaris including Mabruki, a veteran of previous expeditions with Stanley, Livingstone, Burton, and Speke.

The circumnavigation of Victoria Nyanza had been relatively easy compared to what was to come. Yet when Stanley weighed himself, he found he had lost seventy-three pounds. He was then laid low with three attacks of fever, which reduced his weight even further. However, he would not stop. He was determined to return to Uganda and enlist Mtesa's help in continuing the expedition. Stanley purchased a number of canoes to carry his men and supplies across the lake, but the men were inexperienced and progress was painfully slow.

They were trying to reach a group of small islands, but were delayed by strong winds and found themselves still far from their destination when darkness fell. Some of the canoes turned out to be rotten, and one by one they began to break apart, dumping terrified men into the water and sending supplies to the bottom. The *Lady Alice* and the sound canoes reached the islets, unloaded, and rushed back to pick up those in the water. No lives were lost, but five canoes had broken up, and a case of ammunition, twelve hundred pounds of grain, and, worst of all, five guns were at the bottom of the lake. The loss of the canoes slowed the pace of the expedition. Stanley now had to move his supplies in stages. He would paddle the canoes to a suitable resting spot, unload, and then send them back for the remainder of the supplies. One of the resting spots turned out to be a small island just eight miles from the extremely unfriendly isle of Bumbireh.

The people of Bumbireh had many enemies among the tribes in the area, and from them Stanley heard that he was going to be attacked. This time he decided he would not wait. He gathered his askaris along with fighting men from other tribes and rowed over to Bumbireh where the islanders waited on the shore shouting threats and insults. Stanley ordered his men to fire into the crowd. It was a slaughter, and Stanley was later widely criticized for it.

Stanley hoped to enlist Mtesa's aid in exploring what he believed to be Lake Albert, but he found Mtesa embroiled in a serious war against a large rebellious tribe. Stanley was detained for nearly two months. He used the time to continue to persuade Mtesa to convert to Christianity and incidentally help him defeat the rebels. By the time the campaign was over, Mtesa and his entire court had been converted, at least nominally, to the Christian religion. When word of this reached England, there was a surge of missionary activity, and missionaries for Uganda arrived in Africa months before Stanley even completed his explorations.

Even with the help of the king of Uganda, Stanley's plan to explore Lake Albert had to be abandoned. In the first place the body of water that he had believed to be Lake Albert turned out to be an entirely different and much smaller lake. The people of the area were numerous and hostile, and the Ugandan warriors were not particularly trustworthy. Stanley decided to waste no more time; he turned his attention to Lake Tanganyika. On March 27, 1876 the Anglo-American Expedition arrived at Ujiji, where Stanley had had his historic meeting with Livingstone five years before.

Stanley in the *Lady Alice* made a fifty-five day circumnavigation of the lake, which turned out to be the longest freshwater lake in the world. The trip proved conclusively that Burton was wrong; Lake Tanganyika had nothing whatever to do with the source of the Nile. Aside from a few storms, the trip was uneventful.

"There now remained," wrote Stanley, "the grandest task of all, in attempting to settle which Livingstone had sacrificed himself. Is the Lualaba, which he had traced along a course of nearly thirteen hundred miles, the Nile, the Niger, or the Congo? He himself believed it to be the Nile, though a suspicion would intrude itself that it was the Congo."

It was to be an expedition into the least known, wildest, and most dangerous part of Africa. Livingstone had never been able to get his men to go farther than the town of Nyangwe. Stanley proposed to use Nyangwe as his starting point.

CHAPTER 8

The River

Stanley's expedition had already accomplished much. He could have honorably chosen to explore an easier territory to the south and still claim to have accomplished most of what he had originally set out to do. But finishing Livingstone's work and proving that the Lualaba was really the Nile obsessed him, though at first he didn't let on that he had already made up his mind as to what he intended to do.

He asked Frank Pocock to toss a coin to decide. He gave Pocock an Indian rupee. "Heads for the north and the Lualaba; tails for the south and Katanga." The coin came up tails, not just three times but six times running. Stanley didn't like that result, so he decided to draw straws: short straws for the south, long ones for the north and the river. Only short straws were drawn. Stanley could on occasion be a superstitious man, but he was also a determined one, and on this occasion he decided to ignore the omens. "It's no use, Frank. We'll face our destiny, despite the rupee and the straws. With your help, I'll follow the river."

Stanley didn't have enough canoes or enough manpower to tackle this wild region, and he knew it. The only person in the area who could help him was Mohammed bin Sayed, commonly called Tippu Tib (a nickname alluding to a condition of the eyes that made him blink frequently). Stanley referred to him as a "rich Arab," but he was considerably more than that. He was a slave trader, possibly the most callous and successful the world has ever known. Alan Moorehead has described him as "a gangster of the most brutal kind with all the attributes of a scholarly and distinguished gentleman." Tippu Tib had been born on Zanzibar around 1832. His father had been a slave trader and ivory trader. He had simply gone into the family business and had pursued it with extraordinary success. The majority of the slaves passed through Zanzibar, bound for other Arab lands.

Unlike Stanley, who was an explorer in a hurry, slavers usually moved slowly. As Tippu Tib told Stanley, "We travel little by little to get ivory and slaves, and are years about it. It is now nine years since I left Zanzibar." Tippu Tib had gained control over a large district known as Manyuema, and he ruled it like a prince. The tribes of the region became the slaver's private army.

White men interested the slaver. He had helped Livingstone, though Livingstone was an outspoken opponent of slavery. He had aided Verney Lovett Cameron, the first European to cross the African continent, and he was ready to help the even more interesting Mr.

Stanley, for a price, of course. Tippu Tib had one of his men tell Stanley about the country he proposed to enter:

> There are fearfully large boa-constrictors, in the forest of Uregga, suspended by their tails, waiting to gobble up travelers and stray animals. The ants in that forest are not to be despised. You cannot travel without being covered by them and they sting like wasps. There are leopards in countless numbers. . . . Gorillas haunt the woods in legions, and woe befall the man or woman they meet; they run and fasten their fangs in the hands, and bite the fingers one by one, and spit them out one after another. The people are man-eaters. It is nothing but constant fighting. . . . If we go by river, there are falls after falls. Ah, sir, the country is bad, and we have given up trying to trade in that direction.

By having his men pass this story on, Tippu Tib may simply have been trying to raise his fee, but while there was some exaggeration, particularly about the gorillas, the account contained a great deal of truth. Still, Tippu Tib agreed to take seven hundred of his men and accompany the expedition partway down the river for a fee of five thousand dollars.

The expedition marched out of Nyangwe on November 5, 1876. The first day of marching was easy, but on the second they entered the forbidding Mitamba forest. The overhanging trees nearly blotted out the sun and constantly dripped moisture. "As we struggled on through the mud, the perspiration exuded from every pore. Our clothes were soon wet and heavy, with sweat and the fine vapoury rain. Every few minutes we crossed ditches filled with water. . . . Our usual orderly line was therefore soon broken; the column was miles in length. Every man required room to sprawl, and crawl, and scramble as best he could, and every fibre and muscle was required for that purpose."

Even the determined Stanley was becoming discouraged. "I had certainly seen forests before, but all others, compared to this were mere faggots. It appalled the stoutest heart; it disgusted me with its slush and reek, its gloom and monotony." Tippu Tib had begun to regret the bargain he had made, and asked to be allowed to turn back. After a great deal of cajoling Stanley got him to agree to twenty more marches.

Up to this point the *Lady Alice* had been carried overland in sections. But the boat had become increasingly difficult to carry through the jungle, and Stanley decided to launch her. Thus the expedition was divided into two parts. Stanley and the crew of the *Lady Alice* would scout down the river, while Tippu Tib and the majority of the men would follow more slowly on land.

"On our way to [the river], we came to a village, whose sole street was adorned with one hundred and eighty-six skulls, laid in two parallel lines. The natives declared them to be the skulls of gorillas. . . ." When he returned to Europe, Stanley showed one of the skulls to the celebrated professor Thomas Henry Huxley, who declared it to be human.

On November 19 the *Lady Alice* was launched into the Lualaba. For several days all was peaceful, though Stanley knew that the expedition was being carefully watched by concealed men on the shore. Stanley had scrupulously refrained from any hostile act against the tribes that lived along the river, hoping that he would be able to establish friendly relations with them. But they remained suspicious, and with their reputation for hostility, Stanley felt that it would only be a matter of time until they attacked. Stanley never considered that the hostility might have been due in part to the existence of Tippu Tib's slave-trading headquarters nearby and to the fact that he was accompanied by the slaver himself. Only ferocious resistance had kept the slave traders out of this part of Africa. Stanley was puzzled by the "wild rancour of the river tribes and their unreasonable hatred of strangers." He put this behavior down to what he thought were their savage and depraved natures.

The first attack came on November 25. The advance party had set up camp to await the arrival of Tippu Tib and the land party at the point where the Ruiki River emptied into the Lualaba. Stanley left a small group at the camp and set off with the rest in the *Lady Alice* to find Tippu Tib, who had been delayed. When Stanley came back in the afternoon, he saw that his camp was under attack. The attackers were driven off quickly, but it was just the beginning.

Less dramatic but almost as dangerous as the attacks was disease. Smallpox had broken out among the men, and in a ten-day period twelve died of the disease, and many more were so sick that they could no longer walk.

Some abandoned canoes were found, and the sick were loaded into them, so the river-borne portion of the expedition became a combination reconnaissance party and floating hospital.

On December 18, in a region called Vinya-Njara, the tribesmen launched a major attack. They started pelting the boat and canoes with poisoned arrows from the shore. Stanley then headed for a small clearing where his men were barely able to build a brushwood barricade before they were attacked again. Stanley had only forty men who were well enough to fight. The rest stayed in the open canoes in the river.

Stanley and his men fought off attackers for two desperate hours until dusk, when the attacks ended. But throughout the night poisoned arrows showered down on them. Those who suffered most severely were the sick, who had to spend the night in open canoes. During the night, three of them had died. Stanley knew that his expedition could not hold out for long under these conditions. He set out in the *Lady Alice* for a reconnaissance. About a quarter mile up the river he found a large village. He quickly loaded his people into the boats and prepared to storm the village. This was unnecessary, for the village was deserted. Stanley had the village fortified with a brushwood wall. Surrounding trees were cut down so his forces could not be taken by surprise. Guards were posted, and the sick were moved from the canoes and quartered in some of the huts. Just as these precautions were completed, the tribesmen began a wild attack, but they were beaten back. The night was reasonably calm.

About noon of the next day there was an attack from the river. Stanley estimated that between five and eight hundred men were packed into dugouts bearing down on them. At the same time there was a salvo of arrows from the jungle. It was a well-planned, well-executed attack, and despite the superiority of weapons, Stanley and his men would probably have been overrun if Tippu Tib and the advance column of his group had not suddenly appeared. The attackers withdrew, but they had shown great courage and determination. They would be back. Tippu Tib was in no mood for a fight. His men were exhausted from cutting their way through the dense jungle, and they wanted to go home. This time the slaver would not change his mind. If Stanley didn't come up with something quickly, it would mean the end of his expedition.

That night Stanley and a crew of picked men boarded the *Lady Alice*. Their attackers were camped on an island in the river and Stanley figured, correctly, that their canoes would not be guarded. When they got close to the island, Stanley and one of his most trusted Zanzibaris, Uledi, slipped ashore and cut the canoes loose. They were floated downstream to where Frank Pocock and his men awaited them. Altogether thirty-six canoes, some as much as fifty feet long, were captured. It was an enormous haul, and a great loss to the tribesmen of Vinya-Njara. Canoes were the most valuable possessions of these river people. When they discovered their loss the next morning, they were ready to make peace. Stanley returned fifteen of the canoes and paid for the rest. He also released a couple of prisoners who had been captured during the battles.

Despite the victory, Tippu Tib was adamant about leaving, and Stanley felt that he could now continue without the slaver and his men. With the captured canoes he would be able to put all his men on the water, and Tippu Tib could take the many sick and wounded back with him.

On Christmas Day 1876 Stanley declared a brief holiday. The highlight of the festivities was a foot race between Frank Pocock and Tippu Tib. Tippu Tib took the race very seriously, and though he was older, he won easily. Stanley presented him with a silver goblet.

When Tippu Tib left, not a single one of Stanley's people attempted to desert, but they were not happy either. As they rowed off into the unknown, practically every one of them was sobbing.

"A few weak villages allowed our flotilla to glide by unmolested but the majority dispatched their bravest warriors, who assailed us with blind fury."

The land through which Stanley passed was the

model for the jungle that was later to be seen in a thousand films and described in a thousand adventure novels. Here is how Stanley described it.

> Armies of parrots screamed overhead as they flew across the river; aquatic birds whirred by us to less disturbed districts; legions of monkeys sported in the branchy depths; howling baboons alarmed the solitudes; crocodiles haunted the sandy points and islets; herds of hippopotami grunted thunderously at our approach; elephants bathed their sides by the margin of the river; there was unceasing vibration from millions of insects throughout the livelong day.

The river narrowed, and Stanley and his men heard the ominous roar of a cataract up ahead. Actually it turned out to be a series of seven cataracts covering some fifty miles. The cataracts came to be called Stanley Falls. The boats could not be floated through this turbulent water; instead, they would have to be carried around the falls. This meant that the expedition would have to cut its way through the jungle and risk attack from any hostile residents. Getting past the seven cataracts took twenty-two days of carrying and fighting. Stanley's men had to cut a path through the jungle in order to move the large canoes. At every possible spot, they tried to get canoes back into the water even for a short distance, so that they would not have to be carried. This proved to be a mistake, for several canoes were swept over falls and destroyed, but no lives were lost.

There were other hardships. They ran into a swarm of red ants that covered every member of the expedition with painful blistering bites. Stanley said he felt as if his scalp had been raked by a steel comb.

On January 27 the last of the cataracts was passed and

the boats once again entered smooth-flowing water. Here the river, nearly a mile wide, makes a huge curve to the west. Stanley was finally forced to abandon Livingstone's dream, and his own, that the Lualaba was the Nile. If it had been the Nile, the river would have continued to flow northward. The Lualaba was almost certainly the Congo, just as the hated geographers at Brighton had said. Stanley tried to hide his disappointment, even claiming that he had never believed the Lualaba was the Nile in the first place, but the record on this point is clear.

Stanley and his men thought—hoped would perhaps be a better word—that they would have a relatively clear passage now, but these hopes were soon dashed, for the hostility of the tribes along the banks had not abated one bit. The most spectacular and dangerous attack took place on February 1, 1877. The expedition had reached the place where the Aruwimi River joins the Congo. Throughout the day Stanley had heard war drums and war horns along the bank. The expedition was harassed by small canoes. All of this was just a normal daily occurrence. Then Stanley looked up the Aruwimi and saw a fleet of gigantic war canoes bearing down on him. They were far larger in size and number than anything he had encountered so far. He tried to have his boats outrun the canoes, but that was impossible. There was nothing to do but stand and fight. He had his canoes anchored in a double line along the river. The noncombatants, the women and children, held shields around the canoes. The riflemen stood up, took aim, and waited.

There are fifty-four canoes. The foremost is a Leviathan among native craft. It has eighty paddlers, standing in two rows, with spears poised for stabbing, their paddles knobbed with ivory, and the blades carved. There are eight steersmen at the stern, a group of prime young warriors at the bow, capering gleefully, with shield and spear; every arm is ringed with broad ivory bacelets, their heads gay with parrot feathers.

The Leviathan bears down on us with racing speed, its consorts on either flank spurting up the water into foam, and shooting up jets with their sharp prows; a thrilling chant from two thousand throats rises louder and louder on our hearing.

Despite the ferocity and skill of the attack, it was the guns that prevailed. The strain of constant fighting had taken its toll on Stanley's nerves, and he became uncharacteristically vicious. "My blood is up. It is a murderous world, and I have begun to hate the filthy, vulturous ghouls who inhabit it."

Stanley ordered his men to pursue the attackers and chase them from their villages into the jungle. In one of the villages he found a *meskiti*, or temple. It was an impressive structure, at the center of which stood a brightly painted red idol. Covering the idol was a circular roof supported by thirty-three elephant tusks. Stanley allowed his men to loot the temple, another decision that was heavily criticized when he returned to England. The village also contained many other objects of interest, elaborately carved ivory war horns, ceremonial spears, carved stools and masks. This was a tribe of highly skillful artisans. In addition there were a large number of human skulls mounted on poles. This was also a tribe of cannibals.

A bit farther down the river were some tribes that were less interested in fighting than trade, and Stanley was able to get food and a much needed respite from constant warfare for himself and his men. He once again began to hope that perhaps the hostile nature of the tribes along the river had begun to soften. But no, on February 14 the expedition passed the villages of the Bangala, the most military of all the people of the Congo. They were later to form the backbone of the Congo army and police force. Most ominous of all, the Bangala were armed with Portuguese muskets. The Bangala had never seen a European, but for centuries the Portuguese had traded with the coastal peoples of Africa, and some of these goods, including ancient muskets, had made their way to the interior and into the hands of these warriors.

Stanley tried to make peace, but the Bangala began shooting almost the moment they saw the strangers. The Anglo-American expedition was outnumbered and for the first time outgunned. The Bangala certainly knew how to use their weapons, but they did not have the proper ammunition and their guns were effective only at close range. Stanley made sure that his canoes did not get too close, and in the end it was again the superior firepower that prevailed. Stanley rather admired the "ferocious valor" of these people.

In the four months since they had left Nyangwe, Stanley and his Zanzibaris had traveled about 1,200 miles and had fought over thirty battles. Very few professional soldiers have been in as many battles in a lifetime. In every crisis Stanley was decisive and utterly without fear. He was an obvious target, standing up front in the *Lady Alice*. The vast majority of the men on the expedition had been wounded at least once, but not a spear or arrow touched Stanley. He attributed this, of course, to Divine Providence, and to the fact that in a land where no white man had ever been seen before, he was such a curiosity that his enemies always paused for a second look before discharging the arrow or throwing the spear. That hesitation gave Stanley a chance to shoot first.

The river now turned southwestward—it was undeniably the Congo. It was huge now. "It might have been a sea for all we knew." The river contracted again as it cut its way through high cliffs and then quite suddenly emerged into a lakelike expanse, surrounded by white sand cliffs. Frank Pocock shouted, "Why, here are the cliffs of Dover, and this singular expanse we shall call Stanley Pool!"

The worst of the fighting was behind Stanley and his Zanzibaris. The worst of the river was yet to come. Beyond Stanley Pool the river contracted once again and flowed over a series of thirty-two furious cataracts, which Stanley called Livingstone Falls.

To get around this formidable barrier, Stanley had his men work the canoes as close to each of the falls as possible before hauling them out of the water and dragging them overland. Sometimes the canoes got too close and were swept over the rocks by the strong current. One such accident occurred on March 28 just as the expedition was nearing the third cataract. The *Lady Alice* was leading the canoes to a small inlet just six hundred yards from the cataract. All the boats had to stick close to the shore to avoid being caught in the strong midstream current. Most of the canoes arrived safely, but one of the largest was caught in the swift current and went over the falls. Its crew of eight was drowned as Stanley and others watched helplessly. The loss of eight men would have been blow enough, but on board was Kalulu. The death of the boy he had come to regard as his son was a tremendous blow to Stanley. He had already made plans for

Kalulu's future education. Those plans had been dashed to pieces on the rocks of the Congo. Two other smaller canoes were also carried over the falls, though the crews miraculously were not killed. Stanley recorded that this was "the day of horror," and he named the cataract Kalulu Falls.

Accidents continued to occur on the river and the land. The expedition's progress was slowed almost to a crawl. Over a period of thirty-seven days, Stanley and his people had advanced only thirty-one miles. Progress was slowed even more when the canoes had to be carried over a mountain that rose sharply over a thousand feet. Carrying the heavy canoes over this barrier would have been impossible if the local people had been antagonistic, but they were not, and Stanley was able to hire over a hundred of them to help. Still the task took two weeks.

On June 3 Stanley had proceeded on foot a few miles down the river to select a new campsite and if possible to make friends with the local tribes. Passage along the river was blocked by yet another cataract called Zinga Falls. Stanley was looking out over the river with his field glasses when he saw a capsized canoe tumbling over the falls. Stanley and his companions rushed to the shore and were able to help save several who had been in the canoe, but three men were lost. One was Frank Pocock. This was yet another emotional blow to Stanley. Frank had started the expedition as little more than Stanley's personal servant, but he had proved himself over and over again. Frank had been unfailingly lively, cheerful, and optimistic. That was perhaps his best quality. He became Stanley's companion and friend, and he was with the exception of Livingstone the only white man on all of Stanley's African expeditions that he ever really liked. Now this lighthearted young man was dead.

The great tragedy was that Frank's death was entirely unnecessary. He had developed painful sores on his feet and for several days had been unable to walk and was carried from campsite to campsite. The pain and the forced inactivity had made the normally even-tempered young man impatient. One canoe had been ordered to scout the falls but not get too close. Frank crawled to the river's edge and demanded to be taken aboard. As the canoe neared the cataract, the Zanzibaris declared that it was impossible to shoot the falls. Frank, who had been a bargeman in England, thought he knew more about boats than any other man on the expedition. He was also an excellent swimmer and had often said that a good swimmer could not be drowned in the Congo. He challenged the Zanzibaris to shoot the falls. After some argument their response was, "Let us show him that black men fear death as little as white men. . . . A man can die but once."

As the Zanzibaris were maneuvering the canoe across the river to reach what Frank thought was a smooth-flowing stream, they were caught in the current and plunged sideways over the falls. In the maelstrom below, Frank's head had appeared once above the foaming waters; then it disappeared. Eight days later a fisherman found his body floating faceup in the river.

The death first of Kalulu and then of Frank plunged Stanley into the deepest despair he had ever known, and for the first time in his life he thought of suicide. The Zanzibaris too became deeply depressed, more from the exhaustion brought about by the many hardships they had suffered. Some of the men began deserting, though they knew they had no chance of getting home. They declared that they would rather die than travel another mile on the hated river. Local chiefs who were friendly to

Stanley brought the deserters back. They were too apathetic even to run very far.

There was now a new danger—starvation. The expedition had run perilously low on supplies, and the local tribes had begun to demand ever higher prices for food. Stanley could have used his guns and taken the food, but on principle he would not use his weapons unless attacked. There was a more practical side as well, for the news of any attack would travel rapidly down the river and the tribes would either hide their food or attack. Stanley's men were no longer strong enough to withstand a major attack, and they did not have enough ammunition to fight their way to the sea. The Anglo-American expedition had come to resemble a line of hideous walking skeletons.

With starvation came disease, and for some the strain was too much. Safeni, considered by Stanley to be the wisest of the Zanzibari chiefs, suddenly rushed off into the jungle shouting "We are home! We are home! . . . I am about to run all the way to the sea to tell your brothers you are coming." This brave and trusted man had gone mad. A party was dispatched into the jungle to find him, but he was never seen again.

The expedition now really was close to the sea. They had entered known territory. Maps showed that if they continued on the Congo River they would face more falls and rapids, so at the end of July, Stanley decided to finish the journey by land. The *Lady Alice*, which had carried Stanley nearly five thousand miles, was lifted onto a pile of rocks and left to rot.

On August 4, the sick and starving expedition reached the small village of Nsanda. From there Stanley sent a message to Embomma, a major outpost near the coast. He pleaded for supplies that "must arrive within two days or I may have a fearful time among the dying."

Two days later the supplies arrived, and on August 9, 1877, the survivors of the expedition arrived at Embomma and safety, 999 days after leaving Zanzibar. From there they took a steamer to the coast and then sailed by easy stages around the horn of Africa and back to Zanzibar. Of the 359 people who had started with Stanley, only 82 returned with him. Add to that total 6 children who were born on the expedition. Of 36 women who started, only 12 survived. The largest number of those who had died on the march were killed in battles. Smallpox was the second major killer. The others drowned or starved to death or were killed in accidents or by other diseases.

Stanley's Anglo-American expedition was the most remarkable in the history of African exploration, for no previous expedition had mapped so much territory. Two of the greatest lakes in Africa were surveyed for the first time and the world's second longest river had been traced. A large part of the blank space on the map of Africa had been filled in. But the price in human life was very high.

Stanley himself had not come through unmarked. Though he was only thirty-seven, he looked much older.

Despite all the horrors they had experienced while following Stanley, the expedition's surviving Zanzibaris were immensely proud of what they had accomplished and immensely loyal to their leader. On December 13, 1877, when Stanley was ready to depart from Zanzibar, all the surviving participants came down to see him off.

"For me," Stanley wrote, "they are heroes. . . . [I]n the hour of need they had never failed me."

CHAPTER 9

The Empire

At the end of his expedition, Stanley was emaciated and exhausted. He said he wanted a rest; he certainly needed one. Yet resting was not Stanley's normal state. In his mind he was conjuring up vast schemes for the land he had explored.

Stanley thought that the great Congo basin had tremendous commercial potential. There were rare woods, ivory, minerals, palm oil, and other natural resources that would be valuable in Europe. But Stanley was not merely or even primarily interested in exploiting Central Africa. He had the Victorian's faith that material progress would bring moral progress. He wished to "pour the civilization of Europe into the barbarian of Africa," and the civilizing force to which he looked was "the natural and legitimate desire for gain." To Stanley commerce and civilization went hand in hand. His was a faith shared by many throughout the nineteenth century.

From the perspective of the late twentieth century, we can see that such sentiments were often false and were simply used as a cover for ruthless exploitation. Throughout the nineteenth century, European nations made colonies of large sections of Africa in the name of "civilization." But Stanley loved Africa and its people, and he genuinely had a vision of "the transformation of Africa's millions of people from barbarism, oppressed by all the ills of ignorance, superstition and cruelty, into happy and virtuous men and women." Even before he returned to Europe, he had begun to lay out his plans in articles that were printed in the *Telegraph*.

Stanley arrived in Europe in January 1878 ready for a long rest—well, not quite ready. His publishers were pressing him for an account of his epic journey down the Congo—so in four months he completed *Through the Dark Continent*, a two-volume, two thousand page work—then he took a vacation.

He then tried to live like the rich man he had become, primarily from the proceeds of his books and articles. He toured all the famous resorts of Europe but was quite unable to enjoy himself. He was tormented by "morbid feelings." Life without a clear and definite purpose was intolerable to Henry Stanley. So in September of 1878 he abandoned all plans for leisure and went to England.

Stanley was received as a hero. Kings and princes gave him medals and other honors. In the United States a unanimous vote of thanks was passed by both the Senate and House of Representatives. There were some voices of criticism about his attack on the people of Bumbireh and his destruction of the ivory temple. There were ominous whispers about why no white man who set out with Stanley ever came back alive. But these were mere drops of criticism in a flood of adulation.

Stanley was no longer the uncertain upstart who felt he had embarrassed himself in front of the professors at Brighton in 1872; while he appreciated the fame, he wanted more—he wanted to be taken seriously. He went around lecturing not on his adventures but on the commercial possibilities of the Congo Basin. None of the businessmen in Britain were interested in his plans, and there were people who professed to be shocked by the way Stanley appeared to put commerce before religion. Civilizing Africa was the job of missionaries, not merchants, they said.

Over in Belgium, however, King Leopold II was keenly interested in what Stanley was saying, for the explorer's ideas meshed perfectly with his own. The Belgian king had already formed the *Comité d'Études du Haut Congo*, a committee made up of prominent people from different countries that was to study the possibilities of commercial development in West Africa. The king himself was head of the committee.

Almost the first people to greet Stanley when he returned to Europe in 1878 were two representatives of King Leopold. At the time Stanley was interested in working only with Englishmen. Leopold's representatives met Stanley again in Paris in August, but nothing came of the meeting. By November, however, Stanley had become convinced that his plans were going nowhere in Britain, so he went to Brussels to talk directly with the king. The conversations went well, for two months later he was on his way back to Africa. Leopold also headed an organization known as the *Association Internationale Africaine*, which already had an expedition working in Africa. Stanley spent some time advising this group, but in May 1879, he was back in Zanzibar rounding up some of his "faithfuls" for a trip through the Red Sea and the

Mediterranean and down the west coast of Africa to the mouth of the Congo. The project was to be backed by Leopold's committee. Stanley's state of mind at that time can be seen from this entry in his diary:

> August 15, 1879. Arrived off the mouth of the Congo. Two years have passed since I was here before, after my descent of the great River, in 1877. Now, having been the first to explore it, I am to be the first who shall prove its utility to the world. I now debark with my seventy Zanzibaris and Somalis for the purpose of beginning to civilise the Congo Basin.

It was, as one of Stanley's biographers later stated, "a magnificent presumption!" Stanley was working with a tiny crew in one of the most inhospitable regions in the world. He was severely underfunded and backed by no recognized government. Yet Stanley never doubted his ability to complete his task successfully.

The primary obstacle to civilization, as far as Stanley was concerned, were the two hundred or so miles of rapids and cataracts that blocked free navigation up and down the river. Stanley wanted to put steamers into those parts of the river that could be navigated, and build roads around those parts that couldn't. It was laborious, tedious, backbreaking work. Stanley estimated that in 1880 he had traveled back and forth 2,532 miles, in order to complete a mere 52 miles of road.

Since the road would have to stand up under heavy loads in both the wet and dry seasons, Stanley decided that it must be made of crushed rock. None of his men knew how to crush rock, so Stanley picked up a hammer and showed them how to smash big rocks into smaller ones. This simple act earned him the name by which he became known throughout Africa, *Bula Matari*—Breaker of Rocks. More than half a century later road builders in the Congo would still say they were working for Bula Matari.

In addition to the enormous physical obstacles to be overcome, Stanley had endless difficulties with people, particularly with those Europeans whom the committee in Brussels sent out to assist him. The letters he sent back to the committee contained an endless stream of complaints about the officers. Often the men were utterly incompetent and stupid. One man went mad and had to be tied down. Another shot himself. Many were "gentlemen" who didn't really know how to work and refused to learn. Frequently they broke their contracts and simply returned home—over half of them quit before their three-year contract had expired. One man arrived at the mouth of the Congo, took one look at the landscape, and caught the next boat out. Stanley was reluctant to send anyone, no matter how incompetent, back to Europe, because of the difficulty of getting a replacement.

A large number of Europeans returned home in a box; one out of every nine who came out died from disease or accident. The Congo became known as "the white man's grave." This irritated Stanley more than it grieved him, for he believed that if one took sensible precautions one could live comfortably in the Congo. In Stanley's opinion, if you died, it was your fault.

For Stanley this undertaking was not merely a job—it was a crusade to be pursued with near religious fervor. He simply could not understand the others who did not share his enthusiasm and were not willing, or able, to work as hard as he did.

Stanley really believed that he was an easy man to work for: "Being of an open temper and frank disposition, and always willing to hear what my officers or men had to say, though as a leader of men I could not hob-nob with my officers, they ought to have found no difficulty in understanding me."

His officers held quite a different view. One of them wrote: "He treats his white companions as though he were a little king—lives apart, never 'chums' with them, and at certain moments would think it justifiable to sacrifice any one of them to his own safety. . . . You must live with him a long time to understand him. However long you might know him I doubt that you would ever become his friend."

Stanley acknowledged that he was not popular. "I have had no friend on any expedition, no one who could possibly be my companion, on an equal footing, except while with Livingstone. . . . How can he who has witnessed many wars hope to be understood by one whose most shocking sight has been a nosebleed?"

If he was not to have friends, he at least had his mission. "My only comfort was my work. To it I ever turned as to a friend. It occupied my days, and I dwelt fondly on it at night. I rose in the morning, welcoming the dawn, only because it assisted me to my labour; and only those who regarded it from a similar temperament could I consider as my friends."

Toward the Africans, however, Stanley behaved very differently. In Europe some had claimed that he was savage and cruel to the blacks—but those Europeans who worked with him in the Congo presented a different picture. Even the critical officer who had complained that Stanley could never be a friend wrote that "[i]n his dealings with the natives, whatever lies people may say of him, he is invariably kind, merciful, and politic. He can palaver with them. He respects their religions, their customs, their traditions. There is not an atom of truth in the iniquitous accusations of cruelty brought against him. . . ."

With the Africans, Stanley was patient and forgiving. A notable case was that of a chief called Ngalyema. Ngalyema gave Stanley no end of trouble. He sold Stanley land for the road that he did not truly control; then he insisted that he had never been paid in the first place. He was continually making new and different demands. Each time, Stanley tried to deal fairly and respectfully with demands he knew were unreasonable. Ultimately Stanley developed a real affection for the troublesome chief, and the affection was mutual. They became "blood brothers" "with crossing of arms, incisions, and solemn pronouncement by the great fetish-man of the tribe." Their friendship endured for many years.

During the more than five years that Stanley spent in the Congo this time, he made friends with many of those tribes he had fought during his first trip down the river. The difference, Stanley believed, was a matter of time. On his first expedition he had to rush down the river, and the people never had a chance to really know him. "But on this expedition the very necessity of making roads to haul my enormous six-ton wagons gave time for my reputation to travel ahead of me. My name, purpose, and liberal rewards for native help, naturally exaggerated, prepared a welcome for me, and transformed my enemies of the old time into workmen, friendly allies, strong porters and firm friends."

The reason Stanley got on so well with Africans is that he regarded them as children, and he was the father. It was a common nineteenth-century attitude. He was wise, respectful, tolerant—as a good father should be. It was through his kindly guidance that these "children" would be brought to adulthood and civilization. This approach was condescending and unrealistic, and many others were to use such a pose as a cover for the grossest and most brutal forms of exploitation. But Stanley was no hypocrite—that is what he genuinely believed.

Stanley could not adopt this "fatherly" attitude toward Europeans. He was still basically shy and uncomfortable in the presence of "gentlemen." Underneath it all, he remained John Rowlands, the awkward and abandoned workhouse boy who was very much afraid that others would reject him. He protected himself by being rigid and aloof and by setting standards that no one could come up to. Then he could become angry at those who fell short.

Stanley always expected others to work just as hard as he did, and that meant working until they dropped. During his period in the Congo, Stanley often did drop. The fevers that had afflicted him since his days in Arkansas became worse than ever. In May 1881, he had an exceptionally violent attack of fever. Stanley believed in only one treatment, ever larger doses of quinine, even though he had been warned that massive doses were dangerous. He increased his dosage to thirty grains and then was nearly unconscious for six days. When he woke up, he raised his dosage to fifty grains of quinine, but the fever only grew worse. Stanley now felt that he was about to die with his work left unfinished. He was to take one last desperate chance, *sixty* grains of quinine—a kill or cure dose, he thought. But in case it did not work, he wanted to give some final words of encouragement to his men. By the time the Zanzibaris and white officers arrived at his tent, Stanley was thoroughly delirious and almost unable to speak. He cried out, "I am saved," then lost consciousness for two days.

When he awoke, he was terribly weak but felt he was on the road to recovery. During this illness his weight had slipped to a bare hundred pounds. Three months later he declared his recovery to be complete and resumed his work with undiminished enthusiasm. But his strength was not undiminished. In addition to fevers Stanley now began to suffer from what he called "gastric attacks in the stomach." At times the pain was so severe that it drove him temporarily out of his head. Nothing seemed to help these attacks. In 1882 Stanley became so ill that he actually went to Europe briefly to recover.

When he returned to the Congo, he felt that he had been betrayed by those he had left in charge, for much of the work had gone to ruin in his absence. The roads and the boats had been neglected, and the local tribes were alienated and in a state of near revolt. No one else was competent. No one else seemed to care.

Stanley demanded that he be sent a reliable assistant, yet not one of those who came from Europe was even marginally satisfactory. "These people had already given me more trouble than all the African tribes put together. They had inspired such disgust in me that I would rather be condemned to be a bootblack all my life than to be a nurse to beings who had no higher claim to manhood than that externally they might be pretty pictures of men."

There was only one person in the world who Stanley thought could meet his high standards:

> There was a man at that time in retreat, near Mount Carmel. If he but emerged from his seclusion, he had all the elements in him of the man that was needed: indefatigable industry; that magnetism which commands affection, obedience, and perfect

trust; that power of reconciling men, no matter of what colour, to their duties; that cheerful promise that in him lay security and peace; that loving solicitude which betokens the kindly chief.

The man that Stanley praised so extravagantly was General Charles George "Chinese" Gordon. Gordon was a British officer who had served in various capacities all over the world, particularly in China—hence his nickname. He was a strange and isolated man, in many ways much like Stanley himself. Like Stanley, he was a great promoter of European civilization, yet he generally preferred to be away from Europe and in the company of non-Europeans. Like Stanley, Gordon was also extremely religious, and when Stanley wrote of him, Gordon was on retreat in the Holy Land, vowing never to return to the active life. But King Leopold had pressed him to come to the Congo and work with Stanley, and Gordon had agreed until the plan was interrupted by a more pressing call for Gordon's services. This too was to affect Stanley's life profoundly—though no one could know that at the time. Disappointed, Stanley toiled onward, essentially alone until 1884, when he declared that his work was nearly finished.

In a little over five years Stanley had built roads and garrisoned stations for fourteen hundred miles up the Congo. He had established an elaborate political and commercial network among the tribes in the area and was able to claim sovereignty over the land in the name of the committee for which he worked. He had, in fact, established a state. It was a very curious kind of a state, because it belonged to the *Association Internationale Africaine* and that really meant to King Leopold II of Belgium—not to Belgium, mind you, but to King Leopold personally. What Stanley had created was the largest private domain in history, covering nearly a million and a half square miles.

The United States was the first nation diplomatically to recognize this land, which was given the name the Congo Free State (meaning free of taxes). Other countries reluctantly followed the lead of the United States.

Leopold II, king of the Belgians, proclaimed high humanitarian ideals for his new state, though he never visited the land he "owned." The establishment of the Congo Free State probably did do a great deal to disrupt and ultimately destroy the age-old slave trade in Africa. But on every other humanitarian point Leopold's state was an utter disaster. After Stanley left, Leopold's officers exploited and brutalized the people of the region so viciously that there was an international scandal. It was estimated that half the population of the Congo died. Leopold's state was worse than the slave trade.

The Congo Free State existed for twenty-four years, until 1910, when Belgium unwillingly took over the territory from its king and annexed it as the colony called the Belgian Congo. The worst excesses of the Europeans in the Congo were curbed and conditions improved somewhat, but only somewhat. The discovery of copper, diamonds, and other minerals made the Congo a paying proposition for Belgium. When colonialism was swept out of Africa during the 1960s, the Belgian government abruptly abandoned its huge African colony. Though everyone knew independence was coming, the Belgian government, unlike other European powers, had done nothing to prepare people in its colony for the change, and the region was thrown into a period of violent turmoil and bloodshed. Today, renamed Zaire (the African word for Congo), the old Congo Free State is in the grip of a corrupt and stagnant dictatorship. Although potentially rich, Zaire remains one of the poorest, most backward, and badly governed nations on the continent.

Stanley had regarded the founding of the Congo Free State as his proudest accomplishment. He lived long enough to see that his dream of bringing civilization to the heart of Africa had gone badly awry. He believed that the dream had been betrayed by incompetent officials that he had not chosen. In part that was true, but he was never able to recognize that his grand dream was in reality a delusion.

CHAPTER 10

The Sudan

Henry Stanley was to lead one more expedition to Africa. This was to be his most difficult, terrifying, and by all means his oddest adventure. The reason for this expedition can be traced back to the man whom Stanley admired so much, General Charles George "Chinese" Gordon.

In the late 1800s Egypt was officially under the control of Khedive Tewfik of Egypt, but the khedive owed his position to the power of the British government and army, and British officials really ran most of the government. Gordon had been sent as governor general to the Sudan, a vast and sparsely populated region of about a million square miles to the south of Egypt, and over which Egypt claimed sovereignty. Gordon served in the Sudan from 1872 to 1880 and was generally credited with being an able administrator. Since the Egyptians in the Sudan were notoriously corrupt, Gordon appointed a number of European and American officials to oversee the country's far-flung provinces.

After Gordon left, the governmental structure that he had put together began to crumble in the face of a revolt inspired by Mohammed Ahmed ibn el-Seyyid Abdullah, an obscure holy man who proclaimed himself the Mahdi, or "Chosen one of Islam." The Mahdi declared that it was his divine mission to purify Islam and drive the unbelievers—and among them he numbered not only the Europeans but also the Muslim Egyptians—out of the land. His appeal was partly religious, partly political— and astonishingly successful. The British government at first refused to take the Mahdi's revolt seriously, and by the time they did, he had grown so powerful that his army was able to defeat a large, well-equipped force of Egyptians led by a British general, an unprecedented humiliation for the British. The whole Sudan seemed about to fall to the Mahdi and his fanatical followers.

In Britain it was assumed that there was only one man who could save the situation, "Chinese" Gordon. This was the mission that kept Gordon from joining Stanley in the Congo. Just exactly what Gordon was supposed to do in the Sudan has never been entirely clear. Gordon seemed to think that it was his job to organize resistance to the Mahdi; the British government, on the other hand, hinted that he was only to supervise the withdrawal of European and Egyptian officials. Gordon arrived in Khartoum, the principal city of the Sudan, in February 1884—and by mid-March he was trapped there by the Mahdi's army. In London the government hesitated, not wishing to commit a large number of troops, but finally a relief expedition under General Wolseley was dispatched. The relief expedition arrived on January 25, 1885. It was two days too late. On January 23, Khartoum had been overrun, and thousands of inhabitants had been slaughtered, Gordon among them. His head was proudly displayed as a trophy.

When the words "too late" reached England, the entire nation was shocked and ashamed. There were cries for revenge. Yet the government hesitated again, and for good reason. Government officials had never been as enamored of Gordon as the public was. They saw no reason to fight a costly war in a remote and barren territory in which Britain had no real interest just to revenge the death of an eccentric officer who didn't follow orders. So the anger and frustration of the British public just simmered.

Then news began to leak out that the Mahdi had not overwhelmed the entire Sudan and that one of Gordon's appointees was still holding out in the southernmost province called Equatoria. This brave governor was called Emin Pasha. Of all the exotic characters who were attracted to Africa during the late nineteenth century, Emin may have been the most exotic. The name Emin, which means "the Faithful," sounds Turkish—pasha was an honorary title given to high government officials—but this man had been born Eduard Schnitzer, in Prussia. He was the son of Jewish parents, though he apparently was raised as a Protestant. He studied medicine in Berlin and then took off for Turkey, where he became tutor for the children of Ismail Hakki Pasha, and incidentally the lover of the pasha's wife.

When Hakki Pasha died, Schnitzer took his widow and children back to Prussia, leaving them there in the care of his own family. He next turned up in Egypt as a doctor to the poor and made his way southward to join

Gordon's staff in Khartoum. By this time he had changed his name to Mohammed Emin—and nominally become a Muslim—though it may have been a conversion of convenience. "Don't be afraid," he wrote his sister. "I have only adopted the name. I have not become a Turk." Emin also continued to claim he was a practicing Christian. The key to Emin's character was that he had a talent for appearing to be whatever others wished him to be.

Emin worked his way up in Gordon's service and was appointed governor of Equatoria before Gordon left the Sudan in 1880. Emin was no mere chameleon; he had a wide range of accomplishments. He was a passionate naturalist and sent back thousands of specimens of birds and plants to Europe. He was known and respected in European scientific circles. He was a linguist who had mastered a dozen languages ancient and modern. He was a skillful and compassionate physician, who had given his services freely to the poor. He was a fine musician and an excellent chess player. He was, in addition, a reasonably capable administrator of his province. A most unusual man.

Emin's survival, however, was due more to the remoteness of Equatoria than to any skill on his part. The Mahdists had not yet gotten around to it. But the threat was there, and Emin appealed to Europe—and most particularly to Britain—for immediate help.

The relief and rescue of this brave man became, in the minds of a large segment of the British public, a way of partially atoning for the death of Gordon. Since the government was still not interested in throwing men and money into the Sudan, a public committee was formed for the relief of Emin.

The committee was headed by Scottish shipowner William Mackinnon. Mackinnon's motives mixed patriotism and profit. His ships traded with Zanzibar, and he hoped that by involving himself further in the politics of Africa he could gain commercial advantages.

Into the middle of this complex situation the name of Henry Morton Stanley was dropped. When the Emin Pasha Relief Committee sat down to pick a leader for their expedition, Stanley seemed the obvious choice. Not only was he an extremely capable leader, he was so famous that his name alone would attract donations and volunteers. Would Stanley, worn out from his exertions in the Congo, be interested? Stanley was on a lecture tour in America when he was offered the post. He accepted immediately, and on Christmas Eve 1886 he was back in England ready to face this new challenge.

There were two possible routes to Emin's Equatoria province. The first was to leave from the east coast of Africa opposite Zanzibar and return there after contacting Emin. That was the shortest and easiest route, and one Stanley had traveled before. Stanley favored another route. He proposed going to Zanzibar to pick up a force of his always loyal Zanzibaris, then sailing all the way around the horn of Africa to the mouth of the Congo on the west coast, marching across the continent, and meeting Emin on the way. The reasons Stanley favored this rather roundabout route have never been fully known. They may have had something to do with private arrangements made with King Leopold, for most of the march would be carried out in Leopold's Congo territory. This was also the region Stanley had pioneered, and he considered it peculiarly his own. Whatever the reasons, that was the plan that was finally agreed upon, and Stanley set about with his characteristic speed and vigor to organize the Emin Pasha Relief Expedition.

Despite Stanley's ominous reputation for never having returned from Africa with a live white man, he was besieged with requests to join the expedition, though only a small number of men could be taken. Most of those Stanley chose were like twenty-seven-year-old Major Edmund Musgrave Barttelot, a military man who had seen extensive service in Africa.

Others were engaged for less obvious reasons. Arthur J. Mounteney-Jephson was an aristocrat, a distant relative of Gordon and quite inexperienced. He was just the sort of man Stanley would normally have rejected. But Jephson agreed to serve without pay, and his cousin the Countess de Noailles offered to donate a thousand pounds to the expedition. The wealthy naturalist James Jameson also subscribed a thousand pounds for the privilege of accompanying Stanley on the Emin Pasha Relief Expedition.

Stanley ordered a large number of rifles and tons of ammunition, for he believed that this was what Emin would most need. Hiram Maxim, inventor of the Maxim machine gun, donated one to the expedition. Stanley also ordered the construction of a twenty-eight-foot steel boat that could be broken up into twelve sections, each weighing seventy-five pounds, for easy carrying. A catering firm donated forty loads of choice provisions. Some of Stanley's officers may have had the impression that they were embarking on an extended picnic—Stanley knew better.

In February 1887, Stanley was in Zanzibar recruiting the bulk of his expedition from among those people he liked best, the Zanzibaris. He had an important meeting with someone he had known before, the notorious slaver Tippu Tib. In the years since they had first met, Tippu Tib had become even richer and more powerful. He had expanded the Central African area that he controlled through his agents the Manyuema tribesmen. This was an area through which Stanley had to pass in order to reach Emin. Stanley needed not only the slaver's indulgence but also his active cooperation in supplying men to help carry loads for the expedition. In return, Tippu Tib was to get a share of the stock of ivory that Emin was believed to possess, and Stanley would take Tippu Tib and his personal retinue, including thirty-five of his wives, from Zanzibar to Stanley Pool on the Congo. Tippu Tib had business to conduct in that region.

Stanley had another matter to discuss with the slaver. Tippu Tib's people had clashed with representatives of Leopold's Congo Free State. In fact, the Manyuema had wiped out a Free State garrison near Stanley Falls and occupied it. The Free State lacked the forces to recapture the garrison, so Leopold proposed that Tippu Tib be appointed governor of the Stanley Falls area that he already effectively controlled anyway, and that he be paid for the job. All Tippu Tib had to do was fly the Free State flag and pledge allegiance to the Free State and go on doing what he was doing. It was a bribe, and Tippu Tib was delighted with it. He accepted at once.

When news of this agreement reached Europe, there was a general outcry. Stanley had spoken against slavery and always received a great deal of support from antislavery societies and church groups opposed to slavery. Now here he was making an agreement with the greatest slaver of them all. Stanley's counterargument was one of practicality. There was no force in that part of Africa strong enough to crush Tippu Tib, and if the Emin Pasha Relief Expedition was to succeed, some agreement with Tippu Tib was absolutely essential. Stanley pointed out that Gordon, a devoutly religious man, and Livingstone himself had often sought the cooperation of slavers. But Stanley did not really take part actively in the European debate. He was too far away and had his mind on too many other pressing problems.

The Emin Pasha Relief Expedition set out from Zanzibar on February 24, 1887. It was certainly a mixed crew. There were 9 Europeans, 623 Zanzibaris, 75 Sudanese and Somali soldiers, and 97 of Tippu Tib's retinue, including his 35 wives.

Trouble broke out almost immediately. The ship was crowded, and fighting began between the Zanzibaris and the Sudanese soldiers. When the expedition reached the coastal station of Banana at the mouth of the Congo River, the Europeans were dismayed to discover that they would be allowed to take only 180 pounds of personal baggage—this was certainly to be no picnic.

At Banana, Stanley found that the largest of the steamers that was to take the expedition upriver was stuck on a sandbar and useless. There were also all sorts of rumors about a famine along the river, about how impossible it was to recruit pagazis from the river tribes, and about the lack of available boats on the upper Congo. The officers were startled and depressed by such reports. Stanley, who had faced similar situations before, was not bothered. These were simply obstacles to be overcome. He was driven by the haunting fear that his expedition would, like the expedition that had been sent to relieve Gordon, arrive "too late."

More rapidly than anyone could have believed, Stanley arranged the transport for his men and supplies to Matadi, a little over one hundred miles up the Congo. This was the first lap of the expedition. The expedition then had to march around the cataracts over a road that Stanley had spent a year building. On the road the expedition met a handsome wandering artist named Herbert Ward. Ward had been traveling the world and had just spent a couple of years working in the Congo Free State. He was on his way to visit his father in California, but he changed his plans and decided to sign on with Stanley.

The marching was extremely hard. There had indeed

been a famine, and food was hard to obtain. Disease broke out and many men died. The harder the conditions became, the more desertions there were. Pagazis disappeared into the bush, taking their loads of supplies with them. In letters sent home, the officers complained bitterly of the hardships and of Stanley, who was apparently in a vile temper. The officers were beginning to discover what those Europeans who had worked for Stanley in the Free State had discovered; Henry Stanley could be very difficult to get along with, and he favored the Zanzibaris. If there was a dispute, Stanley was usually ready to take the part of the Zanzibaris. One of his officers raged, "It is impossible for any one calling himself a gentleman and an officer, to stand this sort of thing. The fact is, that this is the first time Stanley has ever had gentlemen to deal with on an expedition of this sort." Stanley had dealt with gentlemen before. It wasn't that he didn't know them; the truth was he didn't like them or trust them very much. At one point he raged at one of his officers, "You damned ass, you're tired of me, of the expedition, and of my men. Go into the bush, get, I've done with you." Stanley, who rarely swore, called one of the officers a "God damned son of a sea cook" and a "God damned impudent puppy." Stanley was really furious, but that was the worst language he ever used.

The expedition struggled into Leopoldville on April 21, 1887. They were now 345 miles from the Atlantic and had reached a long stretch of smooth water on the river. They could travel a thousand miles on boats to Yambuya on the Aruwimi River before they had to start marching overland again. That was if Stanley could collect sufficient boats to transport the expedition. It was no easy task, but somehow Stanley accomplished it. This turned out to be the easiest part of the trip, and on July 15 the expedition arrived at the village of Yambuya.

More cataracts blocked further transportation by water, but it was only 350 miles from Yambuya to Albert Nyanza, where they hoped to finally meet Emin Pasha. In actual marching distance the trip was twice as long, and even that wasn't the half of it.

There were not nearly enough pagazis to carry all the supplies. Tippu Tib had promised to send six hundred men, but they had not arrived as scheduled. Stanley, still tormented by the fear that he would arrive "too late," broke his expedition in two. He and four other officers were to lead an advance guard of 389 of the strongest men in a rush to get to Emin. They were to carry a portion of the guns and ammunition, which it was believed that Emin desperately needed. The rear guard was to stay at Yambuya to await the arrival of Tippu Tib and to allow stragglers who were scattered as far back as Leopoldville to catch up.

If Tippu Tib did not arrive in a reasonable length of time, then the rear guard was to make its way forward as best it could. They were to bring as much of the precious ammunition as could be carried. Major Barttelot was made commander of the rear guard. Stanley regarded him as a capable though not a brilliant officer. But he had one fatal flaw, of which Stanley was not aware. Major Barttelot hated blacks—and this was to lead to disaster.

Stanley and the advance column left Yambuya on June 28. Before them lay an unknown region that Stanley called the Great Forest. Today it is known as the Ituri Forest. It was then, and is now, twenty-five thousand square miles of the densest jungle on earth. Trees some two hundred feet high blot out the sun. The floor of the jungle is covered with centuries of rotting vegetation and dead wood. Every imaginable kind of tropical plant grows in this hot steamy environment, as does every imaginable kind of tropical insect and parasite. It was a jungle that contained animals like the okapi, which were known only by rumor in Stanley's day.

Despite the lushness of the jungle it could not easily support human life, and many of its inhabitants were Pygmies—the Mbuti—whose primary hope of survival lay in being able to conceal themselves from their larger enemies and in living in a place so horrible that no one would dare pursue them. The Great Forest was certainly such a place.

Stanley knew the forest was there and that he would have to cross it. He just didn't know how bad it was.

> The daily routine began about six o'clock. After roll call the pioneers [men specially picked for cutting through the jungle] filed out, followed, after a little headway had been gained, by each Company in succession. At this hour the Forest would be buried in a cheerless twilight, the morning mist making every tree shadowy and indistinct. After hacking, hewing and tunneling and creeping slowly for five hours we would halt for refreshment. At one o'clock, the journey would be resumed; and about four, we would prepare our camp for the night. . . . By nine o'clock the men, overcome by fatigue, would be asleep. . . . But during many nights, we would sit shivering under ceaseless torrents of rain.

Progress was painfully slow—five miles a day was considered a good pace under these conditions. Lack of food started to become a serious problem. There were very few villages, and those that were encountered were often hostile or had little food to sell.

"At the end of the first month, there came a change," wrote Stanley. "Our men had gradually lost their splendid courage. The hard work and scanty fare were exhausting. The absence of sunshine and other gloomy environments, were morally depressing. Physically and morally they had deteriorated; and a long rest was imperatively needed. But we could find no settlement that could assure the necessary provisions. Now the blood impoverished, too, the smallest abrasion from a thorn, a puncture from a mosquito or a skewer in the path, developed rapidly into a devouring ulcer. The sick list grew alarmingly large. . . ."

The tribes in the area attacked the expedition, not openly, but by shooting poisoned arrows at them from the dense jungle or by concealing poisoned skewers in the path and around their tiny banana groves.

Whenever smooth-flowing water could be found, the steel boat and the canoes were launched. There was not enough water transport for the entire expedition, so the boats were used to carry some of the supplies and the sick and wounded. In mid-August Stanley, who usually went with the boats, found himself with "twenty-nine men suffering from pleurisy, dysentery, incurable debility, and eight suffering wounds." Even Stanley was demoralized by "looking at the agonies of men dying from lockjaw, listening to their muffled screams, observing the general distress and despondency, from hunger. . . ." Stanley, who was rarely tormented by self-doubt, began to despair. He said, "The dearest passion of my life has been, I think, to succeed in my undertakings; but the last few days have begun to fill me with a doubt of success in the present one."

The horrors of the Great Forest had really just begun. On August 31 a rumor swept the expedition that Emin Pasha had been seen on the river in a canoe. It was not Emin at all but an Arab slaver and his Manyuema assistants. Stanley's expedition had entered an area recently decimated by slave raids. There were no friendly villages to be found, no inhabited villages at all. The men were reduced to eating grubs, white ants, fungi—whatever they could find—and they were starving to death.

On October 6 Stanley left fifty-two of the most desperately ill men, in addition to Captain Robert Nelson, whose feet had become so ulcerated that he could not walk, at a camp that became known as Starvation Camp No. 1. Stanley and the rest pressed on, hoping to find an Arab camp they heard lay just ahead. It was ten days before they found the camp, and they did not receive a warm welcome from the Manyuema, who wanted guns and ammunition for food. These Stanley was unwilling to part with. If he had no weapons to bring Emin, there was no purpose to the expedition. It wasn't until October 26 that Stanley was able to send back food for Nelson and the others. Leading this relief column was Mounteney-Jephson, and what he found at Starvation Camp No. 1 was ghastly. Even before he entered the camp, he saw skeletons. The place appeared deserted. "I came quietly round the tent and found Nelson sitting there; we clasped hands, and then, poor fellow! he turned away and sobbed. . . ." Of the fifty-two left with Nelson, only five were still alive.

The slavers provided Stanley and his men with some food, but barely enough to keep the expedition alive. They wanted to starve Stanley into giving them guns. The Zanzibaris had already sold all their clothes for food, and they now truly looked like walking skeletons. "To add to our desperate state, several of our followers who had not sickened, lost heart, became mad with hunger and wild forebodings, tossed the baggage into the bush and fled from us. . . ." Of all the hardships Stanley had faced, there had never been anything that compared, even remotely, to this trip of horror.

Early in November the expedition entered a less dense part of the forest, and more significantly a part of the forest "untouched by the accursed raiders to whom we owed our miseries." On November 8 the expedition came to the villages at Ibwiri, a prosperous and friendly area. Here Stanley and his men rested and ate the first full meal they had had since August 31. The region "abounded with Indian corn, beans, vegetables, bananas, and plantains, upon which the famished survivors flung themselves, regardless of consequences. Our prolonged fast was at an end, but during the last seventy days of it I had lost one hundred and eighty men, through death and desertion."

The expedition rested and feasted at Ibwiri for thirteen days, giving those who had fallen behind a chance to catch up. Some of the men were gaining a pound a day. It was a very different group that marched out of the friendly villages. They now knew for certain that the worst of the journey was over. Early in December the expedition first caught sight of the distant grasslands of Equatoria from a high ridge. Stanley wrote how, on December 4, they suddenly broke out of the forest into the grassland and into "the unclouded light of a tropic sky. A feeling of exultation immediately possessed me, as if I had been released from Purgatory. . . ."

Now if calculations were correct it would only be a short trip across the grasslands to the shores of Albert Nyanza, where the brave Emin Pasha would be waiting, for surely, Stanley thought, word of his arrival would soon reach Emin's ears. Unfortunately for Stanley, his preconceptions about Emin were to be shattered.

CHAPTER 11

Emin

When Stanley and his expedition stepped into the grasslands, they also walked unknowingly into the middle of a tribal war. The tribes through whose territory Stanley had to pass assumed that he was the enemy and attacked frequently. It took a lot of careful negotiation to convince them otherwise. Stanley was very lucky to find that one of his Zanzibaris had originally come from this region and knew the language. The expedition was now so worn down that they might not have been able to withstand constant attacks.

The expedition finally reached the shores of Albert Nyanza on December 14, 1887. Emin's capital of Wadelai lay somewhere on the other side of the lake. Stanley knew that Emin possessed two steamers and could probably make the trip from his capital in a couple of days. He also was convinced that Emin would by now know of his arrival. There were no telegraphs in this part of Africa, but news traveled quickly anyway. Stanley had hoped that when he arrived at the lake he would find Emin waiting for him. But as he looked out over the water with his telescope, he saw no sign of steamers—indeed there was no sign of a boat of any kind. Stanley asked the people who lived near the lake if they had seen a white man in a boat. Some said that when they were children, a white man had arrived in a "smoking boat." That was probably one of the earlier pashas who had sailed around the lake in 1876. But of Emin there was no news. No one on the lake seemed to have ever heard of him.

Stanley was becoming very uneasy. He estimated that it would take at least a month of hard marching and perhaps fighting to reach Emin's capital. A party could probably row across the lake in four days, but to do that you needed boats. He had hoped to buy canoes from tribes that lived along the lake; however, these tribes never ventured into the water and had no canoes, and there wasn't a tree around large enough for the construction of even one canoe. That meant he would have to go back and get the steel boat that had been left with the wounded and sick in a camp at Ipoto.

For once Stanley decided not to rush madly forward. He simply could not drive himself or his men any farther. Since the area around the lake was barren and the tribes tended to be hostile, Stanley pulled back to the friendly region of Ibwiri and built a fort—Fort Bodo, or "Peaceful Fort"—to use as the base of his operations. The fort was defensible against everything but the rats, fleas, and stinging ants that overran the place and made life at Fort Bodo anything but peaceful.

Stanley then sent a column back to pick up the sick and wounded and the steel boat at Ipoto. By resting at

Fort Bodo, Stanley also assumed that he would soon be joined by the rear guard under Major Barttelot; Stanley was sure that Barttelot must now be toiling his way through the Great Forest on his way to a rendezvous.

As the sick from Ipoto began straggling into Fort Bodo, they told another ghastly tale of starvation and death. Only fifteen of the original twenty-nine had survived. Eleven had died at Ipoto; three more succumbed on the march. The Manyuema chiefs had continued their policy of trying to starve members of the expedition into giving them guns and ammunition. They didn't get any ammunition and men starved.

Just as Stanley was preparing to march back to the lake to seek out Emin with the steel boat, he was struck down by one of his severe gastric attacks. He was nearly out of his mind with pain, and the expedition doctor dosed him with huge quantities of morphine, which barely dulled the pain. It wasn't until early April that a badly weakened Henry Stanley was able to travel once again. On April 19, Stanley reached the village of Kavalli on the shore of Albert Nyanza and was handed an oil-cloth-wrapped packet, which contained a letter from Emin dated March 25, 1888. In the letter Emin said that he had heard of Stanley's arrival in December, and then in March had come to look for him. He advised Stanley to stay where he was, send a messenger, and Emin would come for him.

Stanley was naturally delighted to hear from Emin, but the letter also deepened his misgivings about the man he was supposed to be rescuing. Stanley had driven his expedition forward at a murderous pace in order to bring ammunition to the pasha, who he assumed was desperately in need of it. Yet Emin had delayed for over three months after he heard of Stanley's arrival before even going to look for him. When he finally did set out, he didn't wait around for very long or inquire after Stanley's whereabouts; he just wrote a letter and sailed away. This was curious behavior indeed for a man who was still sending letters to Europe pleading for aid. Stanley dispatched Mounteney-Jephson and a party across the lake in the steel boat to see if they could locate Emin. On April 20 there was a message from Jephson saying he had reached one of the pasha's outposts. Stanley started for the lake at once; by late afternoon Emin's steamer was spotted across the water.

Stanley's meeting with Emin Pasha was not quite as dramatic as his meeting with Livingstone, yet it was not without drama:

> At eight o'clock, amid great rejoicing, and after repeated salutes from rifles, Emin Pasha himself walked into camp accompanied by Captain Casati [an Italian explorer who had been trapped in the Sudan by the revolt and had become Emin's informal adviser] and Mr. Jephson, and one of the Pasha's officers. I shook hands with all, and asked which was Emin Pasha? Then one rather small, slight figure, wearing glasses, arrested my attention by saying in excellent English, "I owe you a thousand thanks, Mr. Stanley; I really do not know how to express my thanks to you."
>
> "Ah, you are Emin Pasha. Do not mention thanks, but come in and sit down. It is so dark out here we cannot see one another."
>
> At the door of the tent we sat, and a wax candle threw light upon the scene. I expected to see a tall, thin, military-looking figure, in faded Egyptian uniform, but instead of it I saw a small, spare figure in a

well-kept fez and a clean suit of snowy cotton drill-ing, well-ironed and of perfect fit.

A dark grizzled beard bordered a face of Magyar cast, though a pair of spectacles lent it somewhat of an Italian or Spanish appearance. There was not a trace in it of ill health or anxiety; it rather indicated good condition of body and peace of mine. Captain Casati, on the other hand, though younger in years, looked gaunt, care-worn, anxious and aged. He like-wise was dressed in clean cottons with an Egyptian fez for a head covering.

While Stanley may have thought Emin looked Span-ish or Italian, pictures showing him with his beard, glasses, and fez make him look, said one writer, like a German doctor at a Shriner's convention. There was an unreal atmosphere to this entire meeting. Stanley the would-be rescuer was haggard and ill; whereas Emin, the man to be rescued, was in perfect health and seemed in no danger whatever. Stanley did not even know whether Emin really needed the ammunition. Stanley very definitely needed the food Emin could supply. The con-ditions of rescued and rescuer seemed to be reversed.

Alan Moorehead has commented, "There was hardly a single quality that these two men had in common. Emin was passive, subtle, studious, indecisive, evasive, meticulous, fatalistic and full of compromise. Before him stood a man . . . who knew only one way of life and that was to march unflinchingly upon his set objectives."

Yet they got on well enough that first evening. Stan-ley brought out five half bottles of champagne that he had saved through all the months of hardship. The party talked pleasantly, and Stanley was not tactless enough to ask why Emin had not come to him more promptly.

The next morning Stanley turned over to Emin such guns and ammunition as he had been able to bring with him, and they began a serious discussion of what was to be done. It was then that problems began to arise. The khedive of Egypt had given Stanley a message for Emin. The khedive said that Egypt could no longer support Emin and his men in Equatoria and that they should probably return with Stanley—however, Emin was not precisely ordered to return. The pasha didn't really want to leave. He hoped that some other government or perhaps some commercial company would continue to support him in his role as viceroy of Equatoria. Stanley had two proposals. The first was that Equatoria be annexed to the Congo under the protection of Leopold; the second was that Emin and his loyal troops set up another Central African state under the protection of the British. Those proposals had seemed reasonable in Europe, but now amid the harsh realities of Central Africa both proposals seemed foolish. They were barely discussed.

Stanley really thought leaving was the best idea and was amazed that Emin did not immediately grasp the precariousness of his situation. Stanley wrote in his diary: "I am unable to gather in the least what his intentions may be . . . but the Pasha's manner is ominous. When I propose a return to the sea to him he has the habit of tapping his knee and smiling in a kind of 'We shall see manner.' It is evident that he finds it difficult to renounce his position. . . ."

Emin raised a whole host of objections to evacuation. He said that such a huge number would have to leave, ten thousand at a minimum, that the undertaking would be too vast. Stanley brushed aside such objections. Then Emin deferred further talk to another day.

What Emin did not reveal was the true weakness of

his position. In Europe he had been viewed as the brave governor who, with a relative handful of loyal Egyptian troops and officials, was holding off the Mahdi's fanatical hordes. In reality Emin's position was not directly threatened by the Mahdi. The real threat came from his own Egyptian troops and officials. He had been reduced to the position of little more than a figurehead and clung to power only because the Egyptians could not agree among themselves what to do, and because they feared that someday the khedive might send an army to punish them if they rebelled. This fear, however, was becoming more remote all the time. Emin had hoped that the arrival of Stanley would quiet potential rebels, but the expedition was so small and pathetic that its appearance had no effect whatever.

Negotiations between Emin and Stanley continued for weeks, with Stanley becoming more and more irritated with Emin's evasions and indecision. Emin wanted Stanley to accompany him on a tour of the military posts of Equatoria in order to convince the soldiers that he had really been sent by the khedive. Stanley just wouldn't do it. Instead, he agreed to have Mounteney-Jephson accompany Emin in order to sound out the feelings of the Egyptians about an evacuation.

Jephson didn't understand exactly what he was supposed to do and wondered why it was necessary to ask people in need of rescue if that's what they wanted. "I think there must be a screw loose somewhere," he wrote in his diary.

Stanley himself and the bulk of his men, now strengthened by some pagazis lent by Emin, marched back to Fort Bodo to resupply the men who had been left there and to see if there was any news of Major Barttelot and the rear column.

It was on this march back to Fort Bodo that Stanley saw the fabled Mountains of the Moon, which he said were "coy, and hard to see" because they were usually buried under "mass upon mass of mist . . . [so that they were] no more visible than if we were thousands of miles away."

These mists or cloud cover are the reason why the mountains, called the Ruwenzori by the people of Africa, are the ultimate source of the Nile. The Ruwenzori range is one of the wettest in the world, and the moisture that falls on the slopes drains into the Kagera River, the main stream that feeds Victoria Nyanza. The water then pours out of the north end of Victoria over Ripon Falls and into a channel that flows directly northward and becomes the mighty Nile. It is the steady rain and snow falling in the mountains deep in Central Africa that provide the water for the river that allowed the civilization of Egypt to develop in one of the driest parts of the world.

While others had rather vaguely reported the existence of these mountains, it was Stanley who provided the first really definitive account of them and who first truly understood the significance of the discovery. He sent word back to the scientifically minded Emin. The pasha responded, "It is wonderful to think how, wherever you go, you distance your predecessors by your discoveries." A flattering statement, but basically a correct one.

Stanley arrived at Fort Bodo, which was in reasonably good order, but the rear column had not yet arrived and even more ominously not a word had been heard from them. Stanley now knew that someone was going to have to march back through the Great Forest and find out what had happened. Stanley could easily have sent one of his officers, but that would not have been like him.

On June 16, Stanley along with 119 Zanzibaris and 100 of Emin's men entered the terrible jungle. The trip was not quite as bad as it had been before. There were no heavy ammunition boxes to carry, the men knew what to expect, and they were more disciplined. But it was quite horrible enough.

Stanley's description of the day of July 25, 1888, is one of the most memorable that he had ever written:

> I was never so sensible of the evils of forest marching as on this day. My own condition of body was so reduced, owing to the mean and miserable diet of vegetables on which I was forced to subsist, that I was more than usually sympathetic. At the time there were about thirty naked [pagazis, Emin's men] in the last stages of life; their former ebon black was changed to an ashy grey hue, and all their bones stood out so fearfully prominent as to create a feeling of wonder how such skeletons were animated with the power of locomotion. Almost every individual among them was the victim of some hideous disease, and tumours, scorched backs, foetid ulcers, were common; while others were afflicted with chronic dysentery and a wretched debility caused by insufficient food. A mere glance at them, with the malodour generated by ailments, caused me to gasp from a spasm of stomach sickness. With all this, the ground was rank with vegetable corruption, the atmosphere heated, stifling, dark, and pregnant with the seeds of decay of myriads of insects, leaves, plants, twigs and branches. At every pace my head, neck, arms, or clothes was caught by a tough creeper, calamus thorn, coarse briar, or a giant thistle-like plant, scratching and rending whatever portion they hooked on. Insects of numberless species lent their

aid to increase my misery, especially the polished black ant, which affects the trumpet tree. As we marched under the leaves these ants contrived to drop on the person, and the bite was more vexatious than a wasp's or red ant's; the part bitten soon swelled, largely, and became white and blistery. I need not name the other species, black, yellow and red ant which crossed the path in armies or clung to almost every plant and fed on every tree. These offensive sights and odours we met day after day, and each step taken was frought with its own particular evil and annoyance, but with my present fading strength and drooping spirits, they had become almost unbearable. . . . I had not meat of any kind, of bird or beast, for nearly a month, subsisting entirely on bananas or plantains. . . . My muscles had become thin and flabby, and were mere cords and sinews, every limb was in a tremor while traveling. . . ."

In addition to the physical hardship was the mental anguish: "My mind suffered under a constant state of anxiety respecting the fate of my twenty choice men which were dispatched as couriers to the rear column under Major Barttelot, as well as of the rear column itself."

The closer Stanley got to Yambuya, where he had left the rear column so many months ago, the more ominous became his forebodings. He caught up with his surviving couriers on August 11. Most of them had been killed or wounded in fights with the local tribes, and the survivors had heard nothing of the rear column.

On August 17, 1888, Stanley finally located the rear column. They were camped in a stockade near the village of Banalya, a mere fifty miles from where Stanley had left them over a year earlier. There was only one white officer left in the camp, William Bonny, a middle-aged ex-sergeant who had been the least senior of the officers, a man Stanley had never regarded as either competent or trustworthy.

The story of the disaster that had overtaken the rear column is one long nightmare. The basic problem was that Major Barttelot had been left in a very difficult position; only a leader of Stanley's abilities could have avoided failure. Barttelot was no Stanley, and he turned failure into disaster.

Barttelot's orders had been to await the arrival of about six hundred men that Tippu Tib had promised. Naturally they did not arrive on time, and the slaver, when he could be contacted at all, gave one excuse after the other. The delay was so long that Barttelot began to expect that Stanley would return before he even got started. He had no idea of the difficulties Stanley had met in the Great Forest or in dealing with Emin. Months went by and the men of the rear column grew restless. To maintain discipline Barttelot, who really hated blacks, instituted increasingly severe punishments; floggings and hangings were regular events. This only increased the restlessness of the men. Disease broke out, there were desertions.

Barttelot heard rumors that Stanley had been killed. He didn't know what to do. Finally, in June of 1888 Tippu Tib sent about 450 Manyuema pagazis. There were not enough men to carry all the supplies, but it was all he was going to get. So in mid-June Barttelot finally started off along the path Stanley had taken eleven months earlier. The Manyuema were sullen and rebellious, and progress was painfully slow, about a mile or two a day, and they had not yet even entered the Great Forest.

The Manyuema women who accompanied the column started each morning by beating drums. This irritated Major Barttelot, and he ordered the practice stopped. On the morning of July 19 Barttelot heard one of the women drumming. He furiously shouted at her to stop. There was a shot and Barttelot fell to the ground dead. Then panic broke out in the camp. Some supplies were lost and stolen. The remaining officers were thrown into near total confusion. One went off to recruit more pagazis. Another went downriver to see if he could reach a station where he might be able to send a telegram to Europe. Bonny was left temporarily in charge. This was the state in which Stanley found the rear guard.

His reaction was utter shock. "I scarcely know how I endured the first few hours. The ceaseless story of calamity vexed my ears. A deadly stench of disaster hung in the air, and the most repellent sights moved and surged before my eyes. I heard of murder and death, of sickness and sorrow, anguish and grief. . . ."

Characteristically, Stanley wasted little time complaining. His first task was to aid the Zanzibaris, most of whom seemed to be suffering from some unknown but ultimately fatal disease. The problem, Stanley soon discovered, was that they had been subsisting on manioc roots, a nourishing food if prepared properly, a poison if not. The Zanzibaris were unfamiliar with the proper preparation of manioc and had been slowly poisoning themselves.

In a little over a month Stanley had reorganized his men and prepared to lead them through the Great Forest one more time. This was the worst land that Stanley had ever seen, and now he had to cross it for the third time. The rear column experienced much the same horrors as Stanley had found on his first two trips through the jungle. In some respects this was the hardest of the trips. Many of the men were already sick and discouraged, and in addition to carrying their own provisions, they had four tons of gunpowder and ammunition that were bound for Emin. The Pygmies still waited in the jungle to pick off stragglers with poisoned arrows, and they still planted poisoned skewers in the path. Starvation was a constant problem. A new threat, an epidemic of small-pox, had broken out among those members of the expedition who had not been vaccinated.

Stanley's mood alternated from a grim, cheerful determination to bleak despair. On October 25 he wrote in his journal, "We are about 160 miles tonight from the grassland; but we shall reduce this figure quickly enough, I hope. Meantime we live in anticipation." But by early December, when starvation and disease had truly begun to take their toll he wrote, "How will all this end? So many have died today, it will be the turn of a few more tomorrow, and a few others the next day, and so on."

It wasn't until December 20 that the rear column broke out of the forest and reached Fort Bodo. Somehow they had come through, but nearly a quarter of those who had started out had died along the way from starvation, disease, or wounds.

At Fort Bodo, Stanley was much relieved to discover that things were in fairly good order except for the constant plague of rats. Stanley had expected that he would find some word from Emin or Mounteney-Jephson, but there was nothing and he was thus given a new cause for anxiety. The only thing to be done was to go and look for them. When Stanley reached Kavalli, he found a packet of letters waiting for him. "As I read them a creeping feeling came over me which was a complete mental paralysis for the time, and deadened all the sensations except that of unmitigated surprise."

The letters were from Emin and Jephson, informing Stanley that in August a revolt had broken out and both men had been taken prisoner by the rebels. Since that time, the letters continued, the rebels had become uncertain and frightened of the consequences of their acts. They had more or less released Jephson, though Emin was being kept under some form of supervision. The letters from Emin were vague as usual. Jephson's was clearer, but still contained many puzzling features as to what had actually happened and what could be done. Stanley, who hated ambiguity, suspected that Jephson had been affected by the atmosphere of evasion and uncertainty that surrounded Emin, that indeed afflicted the entire land. One thing was clear, however; the game was up as far as Emin was concerned. His weakness had been thoroughly exposed, and there was no possibility of his continuing to hold power in Equatoria or anywhere else. Stanley declared that he would now take Emin and as many of his loyal followers as wished to go to the coast. Would Emin agree to such a plan? No one knew.

When Jephson and Stanley finally met on February 6, the officer said, "I know no more about Emin Pasha's intentions this minute than you do yourself, and yet we have talked together every day during your absence."

Finally in mid-February, Emin arrived in Stanley's camp loaded down with his bird and insect specimens and a couple of tons of household goods, which he proposed to take with him. Stanley humored him, yet Emin would still not definitely commit himself to leaving. Should he go or stay with his people? Stanley pointed out that his people had rebelled against him, but then the rebels sent letters indicating that they too might wish to be taken to the sea. This merely deepened Emin's indecision. Stanley, whose life had been one of immediate action, felt that he was being driven mad.

Some of Emin's Egyptian and Sudanese officials and military men began trickling into Stanley's camp. They became troublesome, trying to steal guns apparently with the intention of taking over the expedition. That finally snapped Stanley's control. He stormed into Emin's hut and said that he was leaving at once and Emin must come with him now if he wished to leave at all. Emin began to argue, but Stanley was having none of it. "I leave you to God, and the blood which will now flow must fall upon your own head."

Emin finally agreed. Stanley then had his Zanzibaris round up all of Emin's Egyptians and Sudanese, soldiers and officials alike. While Stanley's men stood by, guns at the ready, Stanley shouted that they were leaving and all who wished to follow Emin must line up immediately. Those who decided to stay behind would be left in peace, but those who chose to march with him must follow his orders absolutely or they would be shot. There was no doubt in anyone's mind that Stanley was ready to carry out the threat.

The Egyptians and Sudanese bowed their heads and prepared to leave. Five days later, on April 10, 1889, a caravan of about fifteen hundred started off for the coast and Zanzibar. There were roughly 230 survivors of Stanley's original expedition and about 600 people from Equatoria. Emin had originally predicted ten thousand would follow him. The rest were pagazis who had been hired locally or the remnants of Tippu Tib's Manyuema.

Relations between Stanley and Emin were strained.

There were moments when Stanley seemed ready simply to dump the irritating pasha. Yet getting Emin out of the Sudan alive was the whole reason behind the expedition, and Stanley knew he would be severely criticized if he abandoned Emin now. Besides, for all his anger, Stanley at times felt a true surge of affection for this strange man.

Emin's emotions are, as usual, impossible to fathom. He probably disliked Stanley and most of the time tried to stay out of his way. Now and then he delayed the entire expedition while he chased after some interesting biological specimen. Hardship had driven him deeper into his passion for natural history. Yet he must have recognized that without Stanley he was a dead man.

The trip proceeded slowly. There was some fighting, but the sheer size of the column discouraged most local tribes from attacking. Stanley was struck with another of his painful gastritis attacks, and for days he was delirious with pain and morphine. Yet, all in all, the long march to the coast was a relatively uneventful one.

On December 4, the column finally reached the town of Bagamoyo on the coast opposite Zanzibar. This was where Stanley had begun both his Livingstone and Congo expeditions. When they arrived, Stanley and Emin discovered that they were heroes throughout the world. In Stanley's case that is not so surprising. Emin's situation was, as always, a bit more complicated. The Germans had been rapidly expanding their power in Africa, and since Emin had been born in Germany, he had been adopted as sort of a German hero in Africa. There was a large company of Germans waiting at Bagamoyo to greet him.

In the strictest sense the Emin Pasha Relief Expedition had been a success. Emin had been rescued, though whether he really needed or deserved rescue is an open question. The cost in suffering and human life had been terrifying—of the over seven hundred people who had started out with Stanley fewer than two hundred people returned. There had been some geographical and scientific profit from the expedition. The Mountains of the Moon had finally been definitely located. But the political and commercial results that had been hoped for never materialized. None of this mattered a bit to the people of Europe and America. The hero Stanley had returned after the most difficult and grandest expedition of his astonishing career. That was all that mattered.

Still, fate was to play one final trick. The evening of their arrival in Bagamoyo, the Germans threw a banquet for Emin and his rescuers on the second floor of the German officers' mess. Speeches were made. Toasts were drunk. It was a happy affair, and Emin seemed happiest of all. He strolled out on to the veranda to get some air and he disappeared. An hour later he was found in the street dangerously hurt. Emin may have had too much to drink. His vision was notoriously poor and he had spent the last fourteen years of his life living in one-story buildings. He fell off the veranda and into the cobblestone street; for days there was considerable uncertainty whether he would survive.

He did recover after a few months, but he never sent a word of thanks to Stanley—a slight which cut the explorer deeply.

Emin elected to stay in Africa working for a while for a German company—an act that the British thought treasonous, since they had rescued him and there was competition between the British and Germans in Africa. Emin traveled to the borders of Equatoria but didn't have the heart to enter. He was now in poor health and nearly blind, and at one point confided to his diary the wish that he had died in his fall at Bagamoyo.

Death was stalking him. During his travels he had broken up an Arab raiding expedition and turned the slavers over to their victims, who tortured them to death. Other Arab slavers vowed revenge. On October 23, 1892, they caught up with Emin near Stanley Falls and slit his throat. So ended the strange career of Eduard Schnitzer, alias Emin Pasha.

Stanley finished up the business of the Emin Pasha Relief Expedition. He paid off his men and tried to sue Tippu Tib for breach of contract. Nothing ever came of it. He then got ready to return to Europe—but felt utterly unprepared for it. He holed up for months in a villa in Cairo pretending to be ill, but in reality completing his book on the Emin expedition entitled *In Darkest Africa* and preparing himself to face the world again.

"No African traveler," he wrote, "ought to be judged during the first year of his return. He is too full of his own reflections; he is too utterly natural; he must speak the truth, if he dies for it; his opinions are too much his own."

CHAPTER 12

Dorothy

The Emin Pasha Relief Expedition made Stanley more famous than he had ever been before. At least in part this fame resulted from the controversy that surrounded the expedition, particularly the rear column disaster. Everyone blamed Tippu Tib. That was the easy part. Basically Stanley also blamed the officers he had left in command of the rear column. He could not forgive them for failing to carry out his orders. The officers, or their families (for the two upon whom Stanley heaped the greatest blame were dead), tried to defend themselves by blaming Stanley. It was an ugly and very public controversy.

Yet the controversy didn't significantly tarnish Stanley's image as a British hero. Although Stanley had long called himself an American (and had actually become a United States citizen in 1885), the British attitude was that he had been born in Britain, and once British, always British. By now Stanley had really come to regard Britain as his home. Ironically, Emin's fame in Germany helped Stanley's image in Great Britain. Since the Germans had adopted Emin, they accused Stanley of practically kidnapping him in Africa. To speak ill of Stanley in Britain seemed to many people to be an unpatriotic act.

Stanley was honored with endless banquets, receptions, and teas. Though he was still a poor speaker, he was much sought after as a lecturer. Stanley now moved with relative ease in society, but he still didn't enjoy it.

He visited King Leopold and discussed future plans for the development of Africa. He was still full of plans. It was assumed that it was just a matter of time before Stanley would return to Africa for another amazing expedition. But instead he did something that surprised a lot of people. On July 12, 1890, just three months after returning to England, the forty-nine-year-old Stanley married Dorothy Tennant, a beautiful, talented, and socially prominent woman of thirty-six, whom he had met some years earlier. At the wedding ceremony in Westminster Abbey, Stanley was so ill with malaria and gastritis that he could barely stand. Only the unbreakable will that had carried him through the Great Forest three times allowed him to get through the wedding ceremony. A doctor accompanied the couple on their honeymoon.

Dorothy Tennant was a minor celebrity in her own right. She was an artist in an age when it was not easy for women to become artists, and she didn't paint teacups or landscapes—she drew nudes. Her drawings of the child beggars of London were published shortly after her marriage.

There was vicious gossip that Stanley, a workhouse boy and a sordid adventurer in the view of some, beat his wife. Bennett even sent a *Herald* reporter snooping around to see if he could pick up any dirt. But Stanley seemed utterly devoted to his wife, and she to him.

They went together for an extended lecture tour of

America. One of the cities they visited was New Orleans—Stanley had not been back for thirty years. He tried to locate some of the places that he remembered, but everything had changed. It all seemed so very long ago. He contented himself with trying to locate "the best cup of coffee in the world" for Dorothy. New York City simply overwhelmed him. It was noisy and unsightly. The man who invented the elevated, Stanley said, should be expelled from civilization, and telephone and telegraph poles in the center of the city were a disgrace.

The couple traveled throughout Europe together, and in Switzerland fate played another little trick on Henry Stanley. The man who had traveled thousands of miles across some of the most rugged terrain in the world without ever once receiving a serious injury slipped and broke his ankle while walking in a placid Swiss meadow.

King Leopold was pressing Stanley to return to the Congo, but marriage and age had changed the explorer. His reply was "We shall see, Your Majesty." He sounded more like the evasive Emin Pasha than Henry Stanley, the man of action.

In fact, he still suffered regularly from malaria and those terrible gastric attacks. He was also now in his fifties, and the fires of burning ambition that had once driven him had cooled. Most of all, with his wife, he seemed to have achieved a certain peace for the first time in his life.

Dorothy was dead set against his going back to Africa, but she was afraid that an inactive Stanley might be tempted to try one more expedition, undertake one more challenge, which might well prove fatal. So she looked around for something to occupy his mind and decided on politics. Her father had been in Parliament, and she had connections. There was no problem about Stanley's citizenship—he had been born in Britain, and now lived there. Dorothy persuaded Stanley to stand for the seat as Liberal Unionist candidate for North Lambeth, London, in 1892. Stanley had a rather haughty attitude about running for office.

"Six or seven years ago I was a different man altogether, but this last expedition has sapped my delight in the rude enjoyments of life, though never at any time could I have looked upon electioneering as enjoyable. The whole business seems to me degrading. I refuse to promise to the people that which I think harmful to the nation. I object to the abject attitude of politicians toward their constituents. If I stand, it is as their leader, not their slave."

He also said, "If I am beaten, I hope it will be by an overwhelming majority, which will for ever prove my incapacity as a candidate." He was beaten, but by a mere 130 votes.

In June 1895 when there was a new election, Stanley ran again. He said that he would be willing to make speeches, but "never will I degrade myself by asking a man for his vote." He didn't ask—Dorothy did all the asking. She wore herself out on her husband's behalf. It was a bitter campaign. The opposition newspapers dredged up all the old stories about Stanley. Stanley still emerged the winner, though not a very gracious winner. When the victory was announced, he was mobbed by his cheering supporters chanting "Speech! Speech!" The short, gray-haired man looked at them steadily and said quietly, "Gentlemen, I thank you. And now, goodnight!"

Parliament was not an ideal place for a man like Stanley. During his first week he jotted down in his journal: "The criminal waste of precious time, devotion to antique customs, the silent endurance of evils, which by a word, could be swept away, have afforded me much matter of wonder." And: "We are herded in the lobbies like so many sheep in a fold; and, among my wonders, has been that such a number of eminent men could consent voluntarily to such servitude, in which I cannot help seeing a great deal of degradation."

His attitude toward Parliament never improved, and when his term was up in 1900 he flatly refused to run again.

Stanley was not an old man, but the frequent attacks of malaria and the even more severe gastritis attacks, which left him doubled up and gasping for breath, were tremendous drains on his strength. His life was running down, and he knew it. In 1893 he started writing his autobiography. He began with sort of a confession:

"There is no reason now for withholding the history of my early years, nothing to prevent my stating every fact about myself. I am now declining in vitality. My hard life in Africa, many fevers, many privations, much physical and mental suffering bring me close to the period of infirmities. My prospects now cannot be blasted by gibes, nor advancement thwarted by prejudice. I stand in no man's way. Therefore, without fear of consequences, or danger to my pride and reserve, I lay bare all circumstances which have attended me from the dawn of consciousness to this present period of indifference."

Yet somehow Stanley found this task extremely difficult. In his early years he was famous for his writing speed, but he labored over the autobiography for years, and he never finished it. He was only able to bring his life as far as the Civil War. Dorothy gathered his notes and diary entries, strung together with her own uncritical narrative, to finish the volume after his death.

In 1896 the Stanleys adopted an infant boy, whom they named Denzil. Unsurprisingly, Stanley turned into a doting and indulgent father. He tried to return some of the affection that he had received from his own "adoptive" father many years earlier.

In 1897 Stanley went back to Africa for one last time, not on an expedition but as a guest celebrating the opening of a railway in Southern Rhodesia. He traveled alone, and found himself missing his wife and child.

In 1899, at the age of fifty-eight, Henry Stanley was knighted. The honor didn't mean much to him anymore.

His health continued to deteriorate. The gastric attacks put him in bed for months. At times he almost seemed ready to give up on life entirely.

During one of his relatively healthy periods Stanley decided that he would like to live in the country. He threw himself into the project of finding and remodeling a house with some of the enthusiasm and meticulous care he had once shown in preparing an expedition to the interior of Africa. The house he purchased was a large mansion in Pirbright, Surrey, about thirty miles from London. Stanley modernized the place, and Dorothy amused herself by naming various parts of the estate after places Stanley had explored: a small lake became Stanley Pool, a stream was named the Congo, a tiny hill was called the Mountains of the Moon. By 1900 the house had been completely rebuilt, yet Stanley kept making changes and improvements. It was the last great project of his life. Perhaps something of his days of starving in Africa or even earlier came back to him, for he had the house stocked with enough provisions to withstand a long siege.

On April 17, 1903, Stanley had a stroke that left him paralyzed. For months he was practically helpless and barely able to speak. By autumn he had regained his speech and was able to walk a bit, but as he had predicted, "the period of infirmities" was upon him. Almost exactly a year later he came down with a serious attack of pleurisy. He knew that he was dying. He asked Dorothy, "Where will they put me? When I am—gone?"

"Stanley, I want to be near you," she said, "but they will put your body in Westminster Abbey."

He smiled and said, "Yes, where we were married; they will put me beside Livingstone, because it is *right* to do so!"

On the morning of May 10, 1904, Henry Morton Stanley, age sixty-three, died.

Funeral services were held in Westminster Abbey, but the Reverend Joseph A. Robinson, dean of Westminster, refused to allow Stanley to be buried there, because he felt Stanley had not done enough to be laid to rest among the nation's heroes. He was only the greatest explorer of his or any other day. He had only solved the most fascinating geographical puzzle in history by locating the sources of the Nile. One wonders what else he had to do? Yet in death Stanley remained the outsider he had been for most of his life.

Dorothy was extremely bitter over this refusal. She had Stanley's body cremated and taken back to the churchyard in the village of Pirbright.

She would have no ordinary headstone for this extraordinary man. She finally found what she wanted, a twelve-foot high, six-ton block of rough granite "fashioned by the ages and colored by time." She had a simple inscription cut deeply into the face of the monolith.

**HENRY MORTON
STANLEY
BULA MATARI
1841–1904
AFRICA**

Bibliography

Anstruther, Ian. *Dr. Livingstone, I Presume?* New York: E. P. Dutton, 1956.

Benét, Laura. *Stanley, Invincible Explorer.* New York: Dodd, Mead, 1955.

Feather, A. G. *Stanley's Story, or Through the Wilds of Africa.* John E. Potter & Co., 1890. Reprint. Chicago: Afro-American Press, 1969.

Farwell, Byron. *The Man Who Presumed.* London: Longmans, Green & Co., 1957.

Davidson, Basil. *Africa in History.* New York: Macmillan, 1968.

Jeal, Tim. *Livingstone.* New York: G. P. Putnam's Sons, 1973.

July, Robert W. *A History of the African People.* New York: Charles Scribner's Sons, 1970.

Keltite, J. Scott, ed. *The Story of Emin's Rescue As Told in Stanley's Letters.* New York: Harper, 1890. Reprint. New York: Negro University Press, 1969.

Moorehead, Alan. *The Blue Nile*. New York: Harper and Row, 1962.

———. *The White Nile*. New York: Harper and Row, 1960.

Stanley, Henry M. *The Congo and the Founding of the Free State*. 2 vols. New York: Harper, 1885.

———. *How I Found Livingstone*. New York: Scribner, Armstrong & Co., 1872. Reprint. New York: Arno Press, 1970.

———. *In Darkest Africa*. 2 vols. New York: Scribner's, 1890.

———. *My Early Travels and Adventures in America*. London: S. Low, Marston, 1895. Reprint. Omaha: University of Nebraska Press, 1982.

———. *My Kalulu*. New York: Scribner's, 1874.

———. *Through the Dark Continent*. 2 vols. New York: Harper, 1878.

Stanley, Henry M., and Stanley, Dorothy. *The Autobiography of Sir Henry Morton Stanley*. Boston: Houghton Mifflin, 1909.

Seitz, Don C. *The James Gordon Bennetts*. Indianapolis: Bobbs-Merrill, 1928.

Index

173